HORIZON

SUMMER, 1973 · VOLUME XV, NUMBER 3

ᴄHORIZON

SUMMER, 1973 · VOLUME XV, NUMBER 3

EDITOR IN CHIEF
Joseph J. Thorndike

EDITOR
Charles L. Mee, Jr.
MANAGING EDITOR: Shirley Tomkievicz
ART DIRECTOR: Kenneth Munowitz
ARTICLES EDITOR: Ormonde de Kay, Jr.
ASSOCIATE EDITORS: Mary Sherman Parsons, Priscilla Flood
CONTRIBUTING EDITORS: Walter Karp, Barbara Klaw
ASSISTANT EDITORS: Kaethe Ellis, Susan G. Ferris
COPY EDITOR: Mary Ann Pfeiffer
ASSISTANT COPY EDITOR: Marya Dalrymple
ASSISTANT TO THE EDITOR: J. Muriel Vrotsos
ROVING EDITOR: Frederic V. Grunfeld

ADVISORY BOARD
Gilbert Highet, *Chairman,* Frederick Burkhardt,
William Harlan Hale, John Walker
EUROPEAN CONSULTING EDITOR: J. H. Plumb, *Christ's College, Cambridge*
CHIEF, EUROPEAN BUREAU, Gertrudis Feliu, *11 rue du Bouloi, Paris 1ᵉʳ*

AMERICAN HERITAGE PUBLISHING COMPANY
PRESIDENT AND PUBLISHER
Paul Gottlieb
EDITORIAL ART DIRECTOR
Murray Belsky
SENIOR EDITORS, HORIZON
Marshall B. Davidson
Oliver Jensen

HORIZON is published every three months by American Heritage Publishing Co., Inc. Editorial and executive offices: 1221 Avenue of the Americas, New York, N.Y. 10020. Treasurer: Marjorie C. Dyer. Secretary: John C. Taylor 3rd. All correspondence about subscriptions should be addressed to: HORIZON Subscription Office, 379 West Center St., Marion, Ohio 43302.

Single copies; $6.00. Subscriptions: $20.00 per year in the U.S. and Canada; elsewhere, $21.00.

Cumulative indexes for Volumes I–V and VI–X are available at $5. HORIZON is also indexed in the *Readers' Guide to Periodical Literature.* The editors welcome contributions but can assume no responsibility for un-solicited material. Title registered U.S. Patent Office. Second-class postage paid at New York. N.Y., and at additional mailing offices.

Anthropomorphology

This summer, HORIZON celebrates its fifteenth birth-day, which is an occasion for astonishment, cautious relief, and expansive pleasure. The magazine's birth, childhood, and adolescence have been watched over by quite a number of people, who are vulgarly called editors but who, in truth, have been more akin to anxious, fretful, and sometimes boastful parents and aunts and uncles. They have tried to give the child an interest in music and letters and history—and, from time to time, they have tried, with little success, to give him an interest in such things as contemporary painting and acid rock. All in all, despite some misgivings and embarrassment, the family feels its charge has turned out rather well. At fifteen, the youngster is still curious, still learning, and still very much alive and looking forward to the years ahead.

I refer to HORIZON in terms of the pathetic fallacy, speaking of its birth and youth, because a magazine does have an uncanny way of taking on a life of its own, rather like a character in a good play. And, like a character in a play, it eventually reaches a point at which the playwright can no longer entirely control its destiny.

Over the years, the editors of HORIZON have con-stantly asked one another what they want most to *do* with the magazine, what the readers would like to read about, what would offend them, what would delight them. In some sense, we have stopped asking such questions. We are limited now by a fully formed character, with crusty prejudices and hearty prefer-ences, not to mention attributes like compulsions, tics, and conditioned reflexes. Some of us would like to see the magazine come to terms with that nineteenth-century painter of dogs, Edwin Landseer; others want it to appreciate the aesthetics of John Cage's music, but it simply will not budge. Like most teen-agers today, on some subjects it is very stubborn.

We are having a bit more success rousing its interest in scientific matters (the article "Of Mars, Martians, and Mariner 9," beginning on page 26 of this issue is, we think, the sort of thing in which HORIZON ought to take a greater interest). And although the magazine seems a bit slow and grudging about it, we are insisting that in the future it pay more attention to the history—and future—of China and Japan.

Those bizarre photographs of clowns in a portfolio that begins on page 48, and the story about the vanishing tiger, seem to me somewhat out of character for the magazine, or at least to be quirks of character. Nonetheless, I see nothing *wrong* with taking an interest in stunning contemporary photographs or in the engrossing yarn told by a friend who went to India to search for tigers—and, well, at a certain point you must let a fifteen-year-old go its own way.

We don't for a minute lament this show of independence. On the contrary, we have been delighted that our youngster's adventurousness and enthusiasms in the past year have brought home to us new ideas about how cities originate, have asked us to imagine what an urban civilization without cities would be, to look with fresh eyes at the paintings of Léger and Blake, to find out all about the radical Berkeley city council, and to puzzle over how the modern world ever began.

We are not permissive parents. We will continue to cajole, lead, advise, rebuke, complain about our charge, and, if we must tell the whole truth, we shall on occasion insist that things be done our way. Yet, for the most part we are pleased with the way HORIZON has turned out, we like our magazine, for all its strange garb and habits, and we like to have it lounging around the house, even if it does have some irritating things to say now and then. And, we look forward to knowing HORIZON for another fifteen years and more.   C.L.M.

COVER: The red-haired beauty painted around 1540 by Mannerist artist Angelo Bronzino was Lucretia Panciatichi, a member of the Florentine court of Grand Duke Cosimo I. Despite the perfection of her dress and bearing, there is a disquieting air of unease about her, in keeping with the spirit of the times. That spirit, and the courtly art it produced, are examined by Professor J. H. Elliott in an article that begins on page 84.
UFFIZI, FLORENCE—SCALA

Adam and Eve are expelled from paradise with the directive, so Arnold Toynbee argues, to go forth and ravage the earth. This handsome painting of the por-

tentous event was done by the fifteenth-century Sienese Giovanni di Paolo.

THE GENESIS OF POLLUTION

O_{nce,}
says this distinguishcd
English historian,
man's awe of nature held
his greed in check.
Then God commanded him to
subdue the earth
and encouraged the rape
of our planet

By ARNOLD J. TOYNBEE

For about two hundred years the advance of the Industrial Revolution has been accelerating. At the same time, it has been increasing in potency. In the nineteenth century, its triumphs were applauded by its beneficiaries—though not by its more numerous victims. Within the last quarter of a century, however, everyone, including the beneficiaries, has rather suddenly become aware of large and sinister entries on the debit side of the account.

The manufacture and use for genocide of two atomic bombs in 1945 made it impossible for us to shut our eyes any longer to the truth that technology is a morally neutral instrument for enhancing human power, an instrument that can be put to work either for good or for evil. We then realized that, even if we were to achieve the difficult feat of making it impossible for atomic energy ever to be used again in warfare, its use for peaceful purposes would confront us with having to dispose innocuously of poisonous atomic waste—a by-product of industrial production far more noxious than coal smog or gas fumes.

For atomic poisoning is merely one arresting example of a phenomenon that is older and more general. Since the outbreak of the Industrial Revolution, man has been progressively polluting his environment. He has been using up natural resources, such as metals and coal and mineral oil, that are irreplaceable. And by employing these resources for industrial production solely with an eye to immediate profit, he has been spoiling for posterity those parts of the natural environment that he has not already consumed.

What is the explanation of the improvidence that has now alarmed us and put us to shame? The superficial explanation is that man, like every other living being, is greedy: the capacity and the impulse to try to exploit the rest of the universe is another name for life itself. Man's greed differs from that of other living beings not in the strength of the impulse but in the degree of the capacity. Our ancestors became human in the act of inventing tools, and within the last two centuries we have discovered how to increase the potency of our tools enormously. We have achieved this by harnessing one after another of the physical forces of inanimate nature, from water power to atomic energy. Here, manifestly, we have the immediate cause of both the genocide at Hiroshima and Nagasaki and the worldwide pollution that threatens to bring comparable catastrophes to human life, on an even broader scale.

All this is obvious, but it is equally obvious that it is only the latest chapter of a long and unfinished story. We must push our inquiry farther back. The Industrial Revolution erupted suddenly, but like the explosion of the bombs in 1945, it was the result of deliberate planning. A hundred years earlier, the founders of the Royal Society had set for themselves the objective of promoting scientific knowledge. The Industrial Revolution was the fruit of a century of sustained endeavors along these lines.

What was it that moved the founders of the Royal Society to give this new direction to thought and action? Their motive was their moral recoil from their experience of human behavior in their own lifetime. The condition of England in the middle decades of the seventeenth century was like that of Northern Ireland today: religious schism, hotted up by fervid theological controversy, had boiled over into civil war. The founders of the Royal Society had been horrified neutrals. They had not only been unwilling to take part themselves in the verbal and military hostilities; they were concerned about directing the energies of their countrymen, and the rest of mankind, into new channels in which their activity would be pacific and beneficent. In science they saw a field of intellectual inquiry that would not, like theology, arouse animosity without being able to provide any agreed conclusions. They found a field of this preferable kind in the factual study of nature. In scientific inquiry, people could disagree amicably until they had settled the points at issue by observation or experiment; then this scientific knowledge could be applied to technology.

The founders of the Royal Society were reacting against a perversion of religion, but they were not themselves unreligious, and still less antireligious. Their first secretary and historian, Sprat, was an Anglican clergyman who became a bishop. They did want to break with traditional Christian intolerance and animosity, and in this they were successful. Thanks to them and to kindred spirits on the Continent, the wars of religion were stopped and toleration was established throughout Europe before the close of the seventeenth century. But in combating intolerance and violence, the pioneers of the Enlightenment were not challenging the Christian doctrine about the relations between God, man, and nature.

This doctrine is enunciated in one sentence in the Bible: "And God blessed them, and God said unto them, Be fruitful, and multiply, and replenish the earth, and subdue it: and have dominion over the fish of the sea, and over the fowl of the air, and over every living thing that moveth upon the earth" (Genesis I, 28). Here was Biblical sanc-

God had created the world; the world was his to do what he liked with; he had chosen to license Adam and Eve to do what *they* liked with it; and their license was not canceled by the Fall.

> For premonotheistic man, nature was not just a treasure-trove of "natural resources." Nature was, for him, a goddess, "Mother Earth" . . . The whole of his environment was divine . . .

tion for the Royal Society's agenda. According to the Bible, God had created the world; the world was his to do what he liked with; he had chosen to license Adam and Eve to do what *they* liked with it; and their license was not canceled by the Fall. The tenant who had parked in the Garden, rent-free, was now rack-rented: "In the sweat of thy face shalt thou eat bread . . ." (Genesis III, 19). But as an offset, the disgraced human tenant, expelled from the Garden of Eden and let loose on the wide world, was not prohibited from easing the payment of his punitive rent to God by harnessing natural forces to do his work for him. Genesis I, 28, gave the license; Genesis III, 19, provided the incentive. In 1663, this read like a blessing on the wealth of Abraham in children and livestock; in 1973, it reads like a license for the population explosion, and like both a license and an incentive for mechanization and pollution.

The thesis of this essay, then, is that some of the major maladies of the present-day world —in particular the recklessly extravagant consumption of nature's irreplaceable treasures, and the pollution of those of them that man has not already devoured—can be traced back to a religious cause, and that this cause is the rise of monotheism.

If one has been brought up as a Christian, Jew, or Moslem, one has been conditioned to take monotheism and its mundane implications for granted. I myself was brought up in the same sect of Christianity as Bishop Sprat. But I was also educated in pre-Christian Greek and Latin literature. This preChristian education, which has had a more enduring effect on my *Welt-*

anschauung than my Christian upbringing, made me aware long ago that the religion of my pre-Christian predecessors at the western end of the Old World had been a different kind of religion from monotheism.

For premonotheistic man, nature was not just a treasure-trove of "natural resources." Nature was, for him, a goddess, "Mother Earth," and the vegetation that sprang from the earth, the animals that roamed, like man himself, over the earth's surface, and the minerals hiding in the earth's bowels all partook of nature's divinity. The whole of his environment was divine, and his sense of nature's divinity outlasted his technological feats of cultivating plants and domesticating animals: wheat and rice were not just "cereals," they were Ceres herself, the goddess who had allowed man to cultivate these life-giving plants and had taught him the art.

In the pre-Christian Greek world, the deification of nature outlasted the rise of philosophy. Divinity was inherent in all natural phenomena—in springs and rivers and the sea; in trees, both the wild oak and the cultivated olive tree; in corn and vines; in mountains; in earthquakes and lightning and thunder. The godhead was diffused throughout the phenomena. It was plural, not singular; a pantheon, not a unique, almighty, superhuman person. When the GrecoRoman world was converted to Christianity, the divinity was drained out of nature and was concentrated in a single, transcendent God. It is true that at the level of folk religion the premonotheistic religion of mankind has lived on under a monotheistic veneer. The local divinities have been replaced by saints; but officially a saint, even Mary "the Mother of God," does not rank as a

minor god or goddess but is merely a human being who has found favor in the unique God's sight by having been obedient to his commands.

At the western end of the Old World, nature-worship, the original religion of all mankind, has been overlaid with an opaque veneer of Christianity and Islam, but when a native of the monotheistic portion of the present-day world travels eastward beyond the easternmost limits of Islam, he finds himself in a living premonotheistic world. If he has had a Greek and Latin education that he has taken seriously, the religion of eastern Asia will be more familiar to him, and also more congenial to him, than the Western religion in which he was brought up. For instance, when I visit Japan, I am constantly reminded, by present-day Japanese religious shrines and sites, of Saint Augustine's description of the pre-Christian religion of the Romans.

My observation of the living religion of eastern Asia, and my book knowledge of the extinguished Greek and Roman religion, have made me aware of a startling and disturbing truth: that monotheism, as enunciated in the Book of Genesis, has removed the age-old restraint that was once placed on man's greed by his awe. Man's greedy impulse to exploit nature used to be held in check by his pious worship of nature. This primitive inhibition has been removed by the rise and spread of monotheism. Moreover, the monotheistic disrespect for nature has survived the weakening of the belief in monotheism in the ex-monotheistic part of the world, and it has invaded that major portion of the world in which monotheism has never become established.

In this context, the modern history

and present plight of Japan are particularly significant. Japanese converts to Christianity have been few, though some of them have been eminent; but the Christian attitude toward nature, which continues to be the post-Christian attitude, has prevailed in Japan in defiance of the contrary *Weltanschauung* that is implicit in the Japanese people's ancestral religions, Shinto and Buddhism. Since the Meiji Restoration of 1868, and with redoubled vehemence since the end of the Second World War, the Japanese have been following the modern Western malpractice of exploiting nature, and they have been incurring the penalty. They have been winning wealth by industrialization and have been reaping pollution from it. Both the increase in the gross national product and the increase in pollution have been more sensational in postwar Japan than anywhere else in the world. Japan's present plight illustrates the truth that the evil consequences of monotheism's revolutionary overthrow of the traditional balance between man and nature can work havoc even where monotheism has never gained any appreciable foothold.

This, then, is the nemesis that modern Western man, together with his imitators in countries like Japan, has brought upon himself by following the the directive given in the first chapter of the Book of Genesis. That directive has turned out to be bad advice, and we are beginning, wisely, to recoil from it. Meanwhile, we are confronted by at least three puzzling questions. First, why was there such a long delay in putting this directive into practice? The application of science to technology and the consequent outbreak of the Industrial Revolution lagged about twenty-six centuries behind the probable date of the compilation of the Book of Genesis. Second, why was the directive given in Genesis only acted upon effectively at a time and place in which people were losing their traditional belief in the inspiration of the Bible and even in the existence of the God of Israel, Christianity, and Islam? Third, why is it that only a minority of the Yahweh worshipers—and ex-Yahweh worshipers—has carried out the directive even now?

Today, the Yahwists and ex-Yahwists amount to nearly half the living generation of mankind; they are outnumbered only by the adherents of philosophies and religions of Indian origin: Hinduism, Jainism, Buddhism, and the rest. Why is it only the Western Christian Yahwists who have obeyed an injunction formulated in Israel or Judah as long ago, perhaps, as the ninth century B.C.? The Old Testament has been held to be divinely inspired Scripture by Eastern Christians, Moslems, and Jews, as well as by Western Christians. Why, then, has the supposedly inspired directive been carried out by the Western Christians alone, and, even by them, so belatedly? Above all, why did not the Jews do the job? The Torah is the Jews' own sacred book, inherited from their pre-Exilic ancestors; the Christians have borrowed it from the Jews unchanged and have merely christened it the "Pentateuch," or the first five books of the "Old Testament." Why has it been the Christians, and only one local sect of them, who have acted on the directive in Genesis? And why have they continued to take it seriously at a time when they were beginning to disbelieve in the divine inspiration that had given the Bible its credentials?

The answer to all these questions is that the injunction to subdue the earth was bound to remain a dead letter "until the times of the Gentiles be fulfilled," and this occurred when Western Christian Gentiles succeeded in enhancing the potency of human technology to a degree that gave Westerners and their non-Western pupils mastery over the rest of nature. "Where your treasure is, there will your heart be also." Westerners have put their treasure in the increase of material affluence; they have set their hearts on this; and "verily . . . they have their reward."

We in the West, Yahwists and ex-Yahwists alike, have been obsessed by the pursuit of economic growth through the advancement of technology: we have been taking unlimited liberties with nature because we have been thinking of her, in monotheistic terms, as unsacrosanct "raw material." It should be noted, however, that this obsession has not been shared with other monotheists: neither Jews, Moslems, nor Eastern Christians have been preoccupied with economics and technology to anything like the same degree. The Jews, who have historically made their living as shepherds, farmers, and traders, have played some part in the development of mechanized industry, but this participation has never been particularly prominent. And it is mechanized industry, not trade or agriculture or animal husbandry, that is polluting the biosphere and using up irreplaceable natural resources. The Moslems were ahead of the Western Christians in science and technology in the early Middle Ages, and if they had kept their lead, they, not the Westerners, might have been the first Yahwists to fulfill Scripture by subduing the earth. Among the Eastern Christians, the

"Where your treasure is, there will your heart be also." Westerners have put their treasure in the increase of material affluence; they have set their hearts on this; and "verily . . . they have their reward."

Man needs to reintegrate himself into the nature of which he is, in truth, an integral part, and he can do this only through ecstasy or contemplation—through religion or philosophy.

Russians have adopted Western technology in self-defense since the time of Peter the Great; in our time they have been competing with the Americans in nuclear science and space exploration, but for the most part they have been following the West's lead and struggling to catch up.

In the Western world, the question of where the West's treasure lay, and where the West was going to put its heart, was raised about six centuries before the outbreak of the Industrial Revolution in the confrontation between Saint Francis of Assisi and his father. Saint Francis's father was a precursor of the modern Western businessman: Pietro Bernardone made money; his son Francesco chose to espouse poverty. In this, Saint Francis was consciously following Christ's example, but without knowing it he was also following the Buddha's. Saint Francis renounced the inheritance of a lucrative family business; the Buddha had renounced the succession to the throne of a kingdom; and the motive of each of these renunciations was the same. Material wealth and power were seen to be obstacles to spiritual achievement.

Pietro Bernardone is the prototype of the modern Westerner; his son Francis offers the antidote to the spiritual sickness that modern Westerners have brought upon themselves by having gained the whole world. Saint Francis was, of course, an unquestioning Yahwist, yet the directive of the first chapter of Genesis did not inhibit him from loving his nonhuman fellow creatures. In his canticle he praises God for the creation of all the Saint's fellow creatures: Brother Sun and Sister Moon, air, water, earth, flowers, grass. He also praises God for human beings, who are

patient in bearing their tribulations, but he comes to them last, and includes them in the fraternity that is headed by the representatives of inanimate nature. Saint Francis was a seer: apparently he foresaw the turn that Western Christendom was going to take. He might have detected this in his own father's career.

What can we do to be saved? Modern industrial man has brought a nemesis on himself by dissociating himself from the rest of nature and subduing it by means of his technology. The damage he has inflicted on his habitat and on himself cannot be repaired by using the same tools: technology cannot be enlisted to save us from its consequences. Man needs to reintegrate himself into the nature of which he is, in truth, an integral part, and he can do this only through ecstasy or contemplation—through religion or philosophy.

The way of ecstasy is illustrated by Saint Francis's canticle, the poem in which he expresses his feeling of brotherhood with the rest of nature, which he put into practice in his daily life. The way of contemplation is illustrated by the Hindu conviction that when a human being looks inward, with his mind's eye, and plumbs his self to its depths, he finds that it is identical with the ultimate reality that is in and behind and beyond the phenomenal universe. "Tat tvam asi"—"That is what thou art"—such is the vision that modern man needs to regain.

Put another way, the remedy lies in reverting from the *Weltanschauung* of monotheism to the *Weltanschauung* of pantheism. The plight in which post-Industrial-Revolution man has landed himself is one more demonstration that

man is not really the master of his environment—not even when he is supposedly armed with a warrant, issued by a supposedly unique and omnipotent God, delegating plenipotentiary powers to man. Nature is now demonstrating to us that she does not recognize the validity of the alleged warrant, and is warning us that if man insists on trying to execute it, he will commit this outrage on nature at his peril.

If the cogent evidence for divinity were really power, Dionysus and Demeter and Zeus and Poseidon, who are now reasserting their power, would be more credible gods than Yahweh, for they are demonstrating to man that he cannot pollute soil, air, and water with impunity. But the founders of the less crude religions and philosophies have perceived that the nature of divinity is not power but love, benevolence, and humanity. The Buddha, the Bodhisattvas, and Christ stand not for the exercise of power but for self-abnegation and self-sacrifice. Confucianism and Shinto stand for a harmonious co-operation between man and nature; Taoism for letting nature take her course, undisturbed by impertinent and clumsy human interference. Surely the *Weltanschauung* that follows from these more perceptive and less aggressive religious and philosophical traditions is the one that now offers the most promising hope of salvaging mankind. The injunction to "subdue," which modern man has taken as his directive, is immoral, impractical, and disastrous.

Professor Toynbee, still going strong at eighty-four, has been assessing the role of religion in human affairs for most of his life. His last contribution to HORIZON *was about anchorites (Spring, 1970).*

THE VANISHING SERVANT

Master and servant: for millenniums this has been an intense human relationship, sometimes short-lived, sometimes lifelong, but rarely casual, indifferent, or uncharged with emotion. A few rare human beings can easily play the role of master or subordinate, but the majority find the first role uneasy and the second one unpleasant and irritating. It requires, therefore, strong social forces, combined with powerful economic needs, to keep the master-servant relationship viable.

At one time, of course, it was a relationship that most people experienced, one way or another, particularly in the older societies of Europe and the East, although the servant class was widespread in eastern and southern America during the nineteenth and early twentieth centuries. But now, everywhere, servants are vanishing; a multimillionaire in the Middle West may, on occasion, have to mow his own lawn, drive his own car, fetch his own newspaper, shop for drink; likewise, his wife may have to cook a meal, stack the dishwasher and adjust the thermostat. In any case, servants or no, she would expect to draw her own bath water and dress herself.

What a contrast with a Victorian woman of similar riches, who, seeing that the drawing-room fire was lackluster, would ring for a footman to wield the poker and put on fresh fuel. As for filling her own bathtub, the idea would have horrified her as much as the thought of getting on her knees and scrubbing the floor. No matter what time she might get back from a ball or a party, she would expect her maid to be awake to help her undress. In the 1930's there were still many upper-class Eng-

Standing behind the laundress and the scullery maid are (left to right) the chambermaid, cook, assistant cook, and parlormaid— the staff of one American household, photographed around 1870.

lish girls who had not the slightest idea of how to make a cup of coffee or boil an egg. Within a generation such luxurious dependence on others had vanished, and even in the thirties the servant class was on the decline.

High wages, greater opportunity for other employment, are the quick and trite explanations for the disappearance of the footman, and the lady's maid. But this is not true. Unemployment is high in the United States and in Britain, and still servants do not abound. High wages obviously do not tempt, for the wages currently offered a butler, maid, or gardener are astronomical by the standards of previous generations. Want ads lure servants with promises of free apartments, color television; the use of a car, long holidays, and limited hours—but to little avail. When dining with the upper middle class in England it is as well to know a few words of Spanish or Portuguese, otherwise one has to channel one's wants through the hostess-interpreter. Nor will you find many blacks, or Indians or Pakistanis, in the

role of servant, as desperately poor as many of them are.

What has happened? Why is the servant class vanishing? Why is it that what once was so comfortable and so secure has become alien and distasteful?

The authority of the master and the devotion of the servant were at their most absolute in the earliest civilizations we know of. When Sir Leonard Woolley found the entrance to the Royal Tombs at Ur, he discovered that the deep passage leading to the burial chamber was lined with the remains of slaughtered girls who had been decked out in finery. There had been no struggle. They had sat quietly waiting for death to transport them to an eternity of service to their dead mistress, for how could she manage without them? Nor was this a quirk of the Sumerian kings: the recent discovery of the royal Han tombs with their jade-clad bodies of prince and princess revealed a similar custom. Servants continued to follow their masters through the doors of death even into late Roman times, when an aristocrat would mark his death with funerary games, bequeathing gladiators or some of his own slaves for the killings.

With the disappearance of slavery and, perhaps, with the spread of Christianity, masters no longer held the power of life and death over servants, but there were few other restrictions in the relationship. Samuel Pepys, displeased by an act of carelessness committed by his young maidservant, thought nothing of beating her with a broom and locking her in a damp, rat-infested cellar for twenty-four hours. Even so, servants were better placed than apprentices, who, because they were bound for seven years, could suffer terrible brutality at the hands of their masters and mistresses; they were flogged, starved, and imprisoned, and if they ran away, they were more often than not hauled back and delivered up to their tormentors. Such subordinate relationships could be exploited by sadistic appetites, and in a world full of brutality, pain, and misery, few cared. Occasionally, a particularly brutal master or mistress was brought to retribution, but most went scot-free.

One of the keys to the problem of the disappearing servant, perhaps, is to be found in the treatment of children. Even into the late Middle Ages English families rarely kept their children at home. The sons of noblemen were sent to act as esquires to princes, while gentlemen sent their sons and daughters to noble households to serve as pages, maids, and the like. Poor children, too, were sent off; not all, of course, but thousands were dispatched to slave for the well-to-do. Most of Pepys's servants were children or adolescents; his boy, Tom, who ran his errands and accompanied him on the lute, was but fourteen when he entered the household. His maids were usually very young girls. In earlier centuries in Europe, people married late—nearer thirty than twenty, for men and women alike. So the servant class was largely a youthful class.

This remained true in the nineteenth century, when the population grew so fast that the developing Industrial Revolution could not always absorb it. Indeed, nineteenth-century England probably saw a greater extension of the servant class than any other Western country, for England was rich and had a large population, of which a considerable section was very young. Furthermore, a declining agriculture meant many girls and boys could not stay on the farms. There was no compulsory education and no social welfare. But there was a tradition of servitude for children, and into service they went.

Of course, not all servants were children: the work generated a sense of security and family loyalty, and many were happy to live out their lives in service.

Boys and girls, after all, became servants at a deeply impressionable age. But more important, service provided a roof, clothing, and above all, food in a world that was drenched in poverty and abounded in slums. How else could a poor, illiterate boy or girl acquire the necessities of life except by slaving in another's home? And the slavery could be mild. In big households, duties were rigidly divided and an ambitious boy or girl might rise through the elaborate hierarchy—from pantry boy to butler, from under nursery-maid to nanny, from kitchen maid to cook, or even to housekeeper, and then one had one's *own* maid. In sickness a servant was looked after, in old age provided for. Conditions varied from household to household, but it was terror of the world without that kept servants within.

The world within could be rich and varied, evil or saintly, chaste or passionate, and occasionally, but rarely, dull. For one thing, servants could live their masters' and mistresses' lives vicariously. If valet or maids, they traveled, not only abroad, but to house parties and weekend junkets; in other servants' halls they were known by their master's name and given his precedence—a rich field here, not only for social snobbery but also for easing the sense of subordination that haunts a servant's life. But perhaps the richest rewards in the servant's world were offered by the triangular relationships between master, servant, and the master's children.

The English nanny was, in a sense, the animal mother of the young child: she fed it, cleaned it, spent days and nights with it, and gave it the warmth, the physical affection, that all young animals need; whereas the true mother was, more often than not, an idealized and glamorous creature living in a different world. Indeed, many would argue that nineteenth-century upper-class Englishmen were addicted to working-class girls because all the physical warmth they knew had come from their lower-class nannies. For the boys, again, there could be another odd servant-master relationship: it was from grooms, game-

keepers, and young footmen that the sons of the house learned about sex, and their first attempts were often made on the servant girls of the household.

There was exploitation at all levels, from mistresses tyrannical through illness to masters tyrannical through sensuality or senility. There was exploitation of loyalty and of lust. The servants might be fed well and used kindly, but they were always *used*. And their resentment took its revenge in subtle ways, from dilatoriness to "accidental" breakages to sexual seduction.

The master-servant relationship is rapidly vanishing, and the reasons therefor are complex—as they always are when an age-old human institution begins to crumble. Education of the young is one reason, and the spread of industrial society, with its opportunities, another. The sharp decline of a rural population is yet a third. Yet none of these quite gets to the heart of the matter. Why should there be far more domestic servants in Moscow than in New York? Why did female domestic service continue unchanged during the war years in Nazi Germany and almost disappear in Britain?

These are not easy questions to answer, but one factor may provide the leading clue: the less patriarchal a society is, the less easy its members find it to accept the master-servant bond. The best servants in Europe today still come from regions where the authority of the family and the father is strong—Portugal, Spain, southern Italy, France. And this might help to explain why black men spurn such work, no matter how lucrative. Whatever the reasons—profoundly sociological or superficially economic—the servant class is following the dodo into oblivion.

Today, pleas for help like this recent want ad in The New York Times *may go unanswered.*

IN SEARCH OF
PRESTER JOHN

Here they were at last in the fabled realm that had fired the imagination of medieval Europe. But where was the Prester, and who were these rude natives that came as his emissaries?

In the imagination of medieval Europe Prester John was a potentate without peer. Half monk, half monarch, he was said to rule over forty-two lesser kings and a strange tangle of creatures that included centaurs and Amazons and a race of shrinking giants, formerly sixty cubits tall but now dwindled to twenty. Throughout his realm there was neither lechery nor poverty nor robbery. His palace had walls of translucent crystal and a roof of gems, and no traveler or pilgrim was ever turned away. Every day thirty thousand guests sat down there at a table fashioned from solid emerald and held up by two pillars of amethyst. This table had the miraculous property of preventing drunkenness, and sobriety was essential because the Prester's guests of honor were always clerics: a dozen archbishops at his right hand and a score of bishops at his left. Indeed, so saintly was the Prester that even his domestics were luminaries of the church: his steward was a patriarch, his marshal an abbot, and his cook a prior. Through his kingdom flowed a river that spewed forth gems from a sea of sand; his clothes were of precious salamander skin washed clean in fire; and the neighboring kingdoms sent tributes by the camel load.

Yet amid all this magnificence, the Prester himself remained a humble man. He was content to use the simple title of Prester, the "priest"; and though

The swordsman opposite, a detail from a sixteenth-century ivory, is an African's portrait of a Portuguese. The beplumed knight above, from one of the earliest Portuguese reports on medieval Ethiopia, is Prester John, the fabled Christian king of Africa.

he had a flock of adoring wives, he allowed them to approach only four times a year. On feast days he sang in person before the altar of the blessed Saint Thomas, who had brought the true religion to his land, and his sole ambition was to crush the snake of Islam. At war he mustered a mighty host—including a division of cannibals who conveniently disposed of corpses after the battle—but in peace he traveled his dominions with only a plain wooden cross and a bowl of earth signifying that from

dust he had come and to dust he would return. His death, however, was of no immediate concern, for in his kingdom sprang the Fountain of Life, and anyone who bathed in it was restored to the full vigor of a man of thirty-two. The Prester himself, it was confidentially said, had taken the cure six times, and his real age was five hundred and sixty-two years.

Exactly where his fabulous realm was to be found, no one was sure. Variously, Prester John had been placed in Mongolia, China, and India, until at last he was settled in that part of Africa that lay east of the Nile. From there, out of Ethiopia, came tantalizing snippets of information to clothe the image: reports of a Christian king who was a sworn enemy of Islam and whose court seethed with priests. It was a disappointment that his realm seemed so small, for even on the crude maps of the day Ethiopia looked mortal-sized. But Europe's theorists were quick to find an explanation: they claimed that the Prester had been driven there by the same all-conquering Mongols who had so nearly swamped Europe.

The Portuguese who first went to look for this Prester John were scarcely suitable emissaries for so Christian a king. Many of them were degredados, convicted criminals who sailed to Africa to search for the Prester's kingdom. If they had found it, they would have won full pardon. But the question never arose, for they never came back. A more prestigious expedition tried rowing up the Congo to look for him, but the venture foundered. At least two Arabic-speaking Portuguese travelers eventually got into Ethiopia, but unfortunately for both of them, the Ethiopian ruler was so delighted that he refused to let them return home and the wretched men spent the rest of their lives at his court in gilded captivity.

The medieval kingdom of Ethiopia lay sprawled across the high plateau that later generations would call the Roof of Africa. It was a severe and forbidding region. Settlement was confined to a handful of towns along the routeways, and to innumerable hamlets huddling against the mountains on whose peaks the inhabitants took refuge in time of war. To the eye of the traveler the country had a bleak and striking grandeur, ridge after ridge of mountain folds extending to the horizon, and all the peaks rising to much the same height so that they looked like waves in an endless seascape of rock.

Ethiopia was unique in that she was a long-established Christian kingdom in Africa. Two Syrians had brought the religion to the port towns of the Red Sea in the fourth century, and from there it had spread up into the highlands. The Ethiopian ruler, the Negus, claimed direct descent from King Solomon and the Queen of Sheba, and many of his people held themselves to be heirs to an emigrant race of Jews. Their Christianity was fierce and belligerent. When fortune favored her, Ethiopia lapped down from her mountain peaks and spread out over the lowlands, reaching northeast as far as the Red Sea coast. When conditions changed, and Ethiopia came under attack, she merely contracted back to her mountain fastnesses and the protection of the seven-thousand-foot rampart of the rift valley that formed her eastern frontier.

Here on the plateau, Christianity took on strange mutations and splendid emphasis. An astonishing proportion of Ethiopians went into the church in

Half-drowned in spring rains, pursued by packs of hyenas, the Portuguese expedition of 1520 struggled through this kind of Ethiopian landscape in search of Prester John.

one role or another—as monks or as priests, as traveling mendicants or as lay brothers. Women joined as nuns, and children could be baptized as deacons while still babes in arms. Fanatics performed extraordinary acts of penance, wearing iron girdles studded with nails or sitting for days in tubs of freezing water up to their necks. Religious buildings were everywhere, in the villages and towns, as isolated monasteries on the mountaintops, or like the churches of Lalibela carved underground from the living rock.

The church was a great landowner, and the clerics in government rose to positions of immense power. The entire edifice was founded on a literal interpretation of the Testaments. Drawing upon the Gospels and finding inspiration in the episodes of Christ's life, Ethiopian Christianity had flourished and put forth exotic blossoms in art and architecture, ceremonial and creed. There were the magnificent, sad-eyed wall paintings illustrating the Gospel stories with a fascination for the role of Mary; enormous open-air consecrations at which the Abuna, or archbishop, of the country ordained hundreds of priests in a single ceremony; wild monks, with matted hair

and leather gowns, who fought as berserkers in the imperial army; and mystic baptisms at which everyone, from the Negus downward, reconfirmed his faith by passing through tanks of water.

Underlying this religious fervor were the problems of ruling a warlike and scattered people divided into clans and factions. At the center was the royal court, clustered around the person of the Negus himself. His power was absolute, but in such a turbulent country his dynasty lasted only as long as his authority over the powerful war chiefs. So his court never stayed in one place for long. A great, tented encampment, it moved around the country like royal pieces in a huge chess game, ready to checkmate any rival with the threat of an imperial army. The Negus's brothers, as potential claimants to the throne, were incarcerated for life in a mountaintop fortress, and anyone who attempted to contact them was put to death. Any provincial governor who grew too strong was summoned to court and dismissed.

But Ethiopia was not entirely isolated. Traditionally the Abuna was a foreigner, appointed by the Coptic Church in Alexandria and sent from Egypt. In Jerusalem, too, there was a house for Ethiopian pilgrims visiting the Holy Land, and one or two religious parties had carried on to Rome itself. There was, in fact, just enough contact for Europe to nurse hopes of finding Prester John in Ethiopia. The result, when the Europeans explored in earnest, was a feat of Portuguese knight-errantry that came close to eclipsing the efforts of the conquistadors in the New World.

The first sizable Portuguese embassy to get through to Prester John made a bad start. They landed on the Red Sea coast of Ethiopia in April, 1520, and the local provincial governor, the Bahrnagas, came down to the beach to greet them with an escort of native tribesmen. In his honor, and incidentally as a useful demonstration of their technical prowess, the Portuguese squadron that had brought the embassy fired off a

In this detail of a facsimile of the world map of Juan de la Cosa, published in 1500, Prester John (he hides the second "a" of "Africa") sits proudly among other semilegendary black kings.

MAPPEMONDE DE JUAN DE LA COSA, FIN DU XVe SIÈCLE 2^e PARTIE

broadside. Unfortunately, one of their guns was still shotted, and to everyone's consternation a large cannon ball went whizzing through the group of dignitaries surrounding the Bahrnagas. Luckily, no one was injured. Full of apologies, the Portuguese tried to make amends, only to be greeted with the Bahrnagas's cool reassurance that "no one was safe unless God pleased, and that the ball had done no one any harm." The Portuguese were happily ignorant of the fact that the Bahrnagas's calm philosophy was based on the extraordinarily low value that he and his countrymen put on human life.

The fourteen members of the Portuguese embassy were an ill-assorted group to be representing their country. In command was Dom Rodrigo da Lima. Young and tactless, he was already quarreling with his second-in-command, Jorge D'Abreu, who fancied himself better fitted to lead the embassy. Trying to hold the balance between the two bantams was Father Francisco Alvarez, once a chaplain to King Emmanuel and now the priest with the task of investigating the religion of Prester John. His diary was to be the first account of Ethiopia published in Europe. Lesser figures in the embassy included a clerk, a painter who was supposed to put on canvas the sights that the party encountered and also draw and paint for the amusement of Prester John, a musician in charge of a portable organ (also for the Prester's entertainment), a barber-surgeon, and a number of Portuguese servants mostly selected for their ability to sing mass melodiously. As a gift they had shipped out a huge four-poster bed with blue and yellow taffeta curtains, blankets embroidered with the Portuguese coat of arms, and a canopy that showed an emperor crowning a queen while four men sounded trumpets. Unfortunately the bed did not survive the journey, and so Da Lima found himself equipped with four lengths of tapestry, the original musical organ, a golden sword with a rich hilt, two old short cannon with some powder and shot,

some pieces of armor, and a map of the world. It was a shabby offering for so magnificent a potentate as Prester John.

From Massawa, on the Red Sea coast, where the embassy landed, it was about four hundred and fifty miles in a direct line to Shoa, in the interior highlands, where the Negus usually mustered his court. It took the Portuguese six months to cover the distance. No real roads led inland, only a few rough tracks: from sea level there was a heartbreaking climb to the plateau of Shoa, a laborious journey past baking limestone cliffs, dried-up watercourses, and meager, rock-strewn countryside. It was, in fact, depressingly like the worst parts of Portugal. Only the names were different. The familiar mesas of Iberia were called ambas in Ethiopia; and if— as the embassy later found—Prester John used the most inaccessible crest as a prison for his rivals, he was not much different from those Portuguese who incarcerated their enemies in the dungeons of Aljubarrota.

Indeed, the similarity between the two cultures, Portuguese and Ethiopian, was one of the more surprising aspects of the quest for Prester John. Both nations were devoutly Christian to the point of fanaticism; both were ruled by absolute monarchs striving to bring a proud and fickle nobility to heel; and each looked to the other as a possible ally against Islam. It was remarkable, therefore, that Da Lima's embassy failed so utterly to understand Ethiopia and her people.

Bad luck had much to do with it. Everything went wrong from the start. The hot-tempered Da Lima characteristically offended the Bahrnagas by declining his hospitality; an epidemic carried off two members of the group, one of them the interpreter; and then there was the matter of presents. Da Lima did not understand that all diplomatic business in Ethiopia depended on a constant supply of flattering gifts. Even the doorkeepers of the Bahrnagas's chambers had to be bribed with packets of pepper; and when the Bahr-

nagas asked for Da Lima's best sword, he was deeply offended that the Portuguese commander turned to a companion and borrowed a second-rate weapon for the gift. That night the Portuguese stores were broken into and two swords and a helmet stolen.

For his part, Da Lima was singularly unimpressed with the Bahrnagas. Instead of some grand potentate of oriental luxury, he found in the Prester's lieutenant an ugly-looking rogue obviously suffering from eye disease and seated on an ill-made string bed covered with unclean rugs. His audience chamber was a great barn of a place, packed with rank upon rank of natives squatting half-naked on the earthen floor. To one side attendants held four of the Bahrnagas's favorite war horses, while on a wall near him hung a few poorly fashioned swords. At the head of his bed crouched his wife. Even important men who entered the chamber were first obliged to strip from the waist up, and then bob down and touch the ground with one hand as a sign of respect before giving the obligatory tribute of spice or cloth.

Only Father Alvarez was content. Here indeed, he confided to his diary, was the land of Prester John. Every hill and crossroads sprouted a church or monastery. In the market place the chief customers were monastic bursars; and on the march every second passer-by seemed to be in holy orders— monks in yellow robes that reminded Alvarez of the Dominicans, half-naked mendicant priests, and nuns with their heads shaved and bound up with a leather thong. Alvarez went into the churches to admire the wall paintings and the rich drapes of red velvet and brocade that hid the altars. Only the church furniture seemed inadequate. There were skeins of thin stones instead of bells, which knocked together and made a cracked, tinkling sound; and the clumsy, ill-wrought church plate did little justice to the alleged vast wealth of Prester John.

Conversely, the Ethiopians were taking stock of their Portuguese guests and not necessarily liking what they found.

FINDING
PRESTER JOHN

Although hardly the potentate that the Portuguese had expected to find, Prester John *did* exist as the Negus, or the king, of Ethiopia. No contemporary portrait of this monarch has survived, but his trappings and regalia were probably somewhat like those of "King David," at right, in an illumination from an eighteenth-century Ethiopian manuscript. Arriving at the Prester's camp in October, 1520, the Portuguese waited some time to catch a glimpse of him. At last they were invited to see a mass baptism, like the one at left. The priest (topmost) is standing in a narrow tank in which his congregation is being submerged, including the king at center. In fact, the king was privileged to be baptized by himself. When a witness watched the rite, he was shocked to observe that the priest was as "naked as when his mother bore him," despite the bitter cold.

They admired their fine weapons and armor and begged them as gifts. But when the priests invited their visitors to share mass with them, they were shocked by their uncouth behavior. The Portuguese talked in loud voices and spat openly on the church floor, and they seemed always to be quarreling. Even their holy man was something of a menace, for Alvarez committed the sin of riding up on a female donkey to a monastery where no female creatures of any sort were allowed. Only a hurried deputation sallying forth to make him dismount prevented the entire monastery from being defiled.

Loyally, Alvarez enumerated everything worthy of the realm of Prester John. There were communities of nuns who piously insisted on washing the travelers' feet, royal guesthouses for people on state business, and an occasional chieftain who was courteous to the passing embassy. But for the most part, the people of Prester John were neither hospitable nor decorous. Some of the men strutted about with nothing but a leather strap around their testicles; and women scarcely covered their nakedness, dangling a sheepskin casually from one shoulder. "In Portugal or Spain," Alvarez commented dryly, "people marry for love, and because they see beautiful faces, and be-cause they see beautiful faces, and be-

things inside are hidden from them; in this country they can well marry as they see everything for certain."

But it was the violence of the country that really shocked the visitors. In several villages the natives turned out to stone them, and Alvarez had to send his mule and a slave on ahead to draw any fire from ambushers. At night the guides built barricades of thorn bushes against brigands, and in one place the travelers rode through a wood where the rotting heads of eight hundred executed rebels dangled like grotesque apples from the branches. In the realm of Prester John, it was becoming increasingly clear, tempers ran high and blood was easily spilled. Several times the embassy was left stranded when their porters flung their loads to the ground and marched off. In the middle of one dispute, a high-ranking monk suddenly appeared and sprang like a tiger on the Ethiopian captain of the guard who had been sent with them, beating him about the head. Then he calmly introduced himself as a messenger from the Negus, told the startled Da Lima that the emperor was dissatisfied with the progress of the expedition, and abruptly hurried off.

Scrambling on hands and knees over high passes, harried by packs of hyenas so bold they had to be jabbed away with lances, nearly drowned in a flash flood,

the Portuguese were heartily glad when, in mid-October, their guides finally announced that the Prester's camp lay just ahead. The embassy had long since given up any hope of seeing the legendary crystal palace, so the sight of the massed tents of the Ethiopian court cheered them considerably. It lay like a huge military cantonment, row upon row of tents radiating out from the great, red central pavilion of the Negus. Several thousand Ethiopians, dressed in their finest clothing, had assembled to watch the embassy arrive. They stood silent and curious while a company of a hundred heralds in silk shirts cleared a path for the white men, waving and cracking their whips in the air. The crowd fell back to form an aisle, flanked by the nobles and by the Negus's horses, drawn up as if on parade, with brocade saddle cloths and plumes nodding from their bridles. Next, a double column of imperial messengers ran forward, each man wearing a lion skin thrown over one shoulder and a gold collar studded with semiprecious stones around his throat. Taking up positions on each side of Da Lima and his men, they ushered them along, moving at a curious pace with a shambling half-run, half-lope. The visitors were made to pass between four captive lions, securely held, Alvarez noted with some relief, by massive chains. Finally,

17

In this fifteenth-century manuscript illumination, Saint George rides out, lance in hand, as Ethiopia's patron saint. By the time the Portu-guese arrived, Ethiopia had been a Christian land for 1200 years and possessed as impressive a body of religious art as Portugal herself.

a bowshot from the mysterious red pavilion, the procession came to a halt, and the Portuguese began a garbled second-hand dialogue with the man they had come so far to see.

The go-between was a court functionary whom Alvarez called the Cabeata. Dressed in a white cotton gown and a tall, pointed hat, he acted as chamberlain to the Negus, who remained hidden in his tent. The Cabeata opened the audience by solemnly demanding of Da Lima what he wanted and where he came from. The ambassador replied that he had brought an embassy to Prester John from the king of Portugal and messages from the viceroy of India. At this the Cabeata turned around and sedately marched back into the red tent. A few moments later he came out and repeated his first question. Again Da Lima stated his business. Back went the Cabeata, only to re-emerge to ask his question yet a third time. Da Lima was so nonplussed at this that he replied that he did not know how to reply. As he thought best, was the Cabeata's unhelpful answer.

This retort piqued Da Lima into asserting that he would not deliver his embassy to anyone except the Prester in person, and the answer produced an immediate reaction. On his next appearance from the red tent the Cabeata raised the question of gifts. His lord, he announced, demanded to see all the presents that the embassy had brought him. One by one, the meager collection of gifts was produced; quickly they were picked up and carried into the tent for the Negus to inspect. In a few minutes they were brought back. The Portuguese brocades were hung on a wooden arcade for display, and the other articles were arrayed on the ground for maximum effect. Then one of the Ethiopian nobles harangued the crowd on the great value of the presents and the honor the Portuguese had done their

Like a beached Noah's Ark, an ancient Ethiopian rock church shelters beneath the arch of a mountain cavern. Built around A.D. *1200 near the city of Lalibela, it is still virtually inaccessible.*

lord by coming to see him. When he had finished, the crowd gave a great shout and began to disperse. Da Lima and his companions were left where they stood, aware that their first audience with the Negus had come to an end without their having had a chance to pass on their messages from Portugal.

The Portuguese never did come to grips with the eccentricities of Ethiopian court life. The entire system was devoted to maintaining the mystique of the Negus as a hidden, all-powerful despot. In camp he remained shut up in his tent; on the march he was shielded from the public gaze by cloths held up on poles by his bearers, while lion handlers cleared his path of any stray onlookers. His power was projected as being absolute and omnipresent. No one, from the lowest to the highest rank, was immune from the Negus's whims. The Minister of Justice himself was hauled off to be whipped, and great Ethiopian lords might be ruined in the twinkling of an eye, stripped of rank and privileges and reduced to serfs by the Negus. Even the most senile and feeble tribal chieftains staggered around the court carrying great blocks of stone

in their arms as tokens of submission. But the brutality was softened with unexpected streaks of humanity. A man condemned to be whipped would be marched off by the guards with every appearance of ferocity. He would be thrown to the ground, and a great show would be made of flogging him half to death. But on closer inspection it would turn out that most of the blows were not aimed at the prisoner but struck the ground as a sham punishment. When it was over, the victim got to his feet and calmly returned to the court circle. In Alvarez's opinion, the most intelligent part of Ethiopian justice was that false accusations were discouraged by making the accuser pay the accused's expenses while he awaited trial.

To their surprise, the Portuguese found that there were other Europeans already at the Negus's court, mostly artisans and men who had escaped from Moorish captivity and taken refuge in Christian Ethiopia. Indeed, considering the number of Europeans the Negus must already have seen, it was surprising how much interest he showed in Da Lima's inept little embassy. He was forever sending runners to the Portuguese tents to deliver strange requests. The Negus had heard that the Portuguese were great horsemen; would they oblige him with a riding display in front of his tent? They were asked to send over a musket, or a Catholic cross, or a pair of breeches for him to inspect. Some of the requests—for example, whether anyone in the embassy knew how to manufacture gunpowder—seemed very sensible; others were more frivolous. The Portuguese were obliged to put on exhibitions of dancing, fencing, and even swimming. Probably the oddest request was that the visitors hold a banquet and sing and carouse in their own style; during this observers ran to tell the Negus how the white men behaved when drunk.

OVERLEAF: *The monastery of Dabro Damo has stood on this towering mesa for a millennium.*

But it was Father Alvarez who attracted the most attention. He had come to examine Prester John's faith, but found instead that he was cast as a performing representative of the Church of Rome. A small tent was set up as a chapel next to the Negus's pavilion, and there Alvarez was asked to demonstrate every ritual in the Church calendar. Fortunately he proved quite a showman. He decorated his chapel with all the trappings he could devise, recruited a choir to accompany the organist from the embassy, performed mass, and even borrowed a baby to demonstrate a baptism in slow-motion so that the Ethiopians could ask questions at intervals. The Negus paid the closest attention to everything. Messengers came bursting in to ask explanations of such minor details as a change in the hymn tune, and at night they lit the interior of the chapel with candles and raised the tent flap so that the Negus could watch the Catholic priest in action. This was a situation that Father Alvarez milked shamelessly by flicking holy water from his hyssop across the gap so that it fell on the skirts of the royal tent.

Much of Ethiopian court life took place after dark, to cloak the activities of the Negus still further. Time and again the Portuguese were roused from sleep to answer questions sent by the Negus, and Alvarez had to spend one entire night observing the annual mass baptism of the court. A large tank had been dug and lined with planks and canvas to make it watertight, and then a stream diverted to fill it. A marquee was erected over the pool, and early in the night—it was bitterly cold on the wind-swept plateau—the Negus entered alone to be immersed and baptized privately at the hands of his personal chaplain, who stood chest-deep in the water. After the Negus had climbed out of the pool, he took up his position in a small kiosk from which he could watch the rest of the ceremony through

This cruciform church at Lalibela was carved from a single rock. Unique among Ethiopian churches, it is said to have been built in the thirteenth century at the express command of Saint George.

a peephole. Only the immediate members of the imperial family were permitted to wear any clothing while being ducked. All the rest entered stark naked, much to Alvarez's embarrassment.

When the Portuguese at last saw the Negus face to face, the meeting also took place after dark. It was a splendid *coup de théâtre.* Without warning, the Portuguese were awakened and told to dress. They were then taken to the entrance of the royal pavilion. There they found a thousand of the imperial guard, glittering in coats of mail and armed with shields, swords, and assegais. Escorted into the tent, the Portuguese were brought forward past several sets of curtains, each more gorgeous than the last, until the final set drew back to reveal the Negus himself, about twelve feet away and seated on a platform covered with rich carpets. He was a young man, round-faced and with large eyes. On his head was a tall crown of gold and silver; a brocade mantle covered his shoulders, and across his knees lay a cloth of gold like a bishop's apron. Four attendants stood motionless with candles in their hands to form a spectacular backdrop; while on each side of the Negus were men with drawn swords, and at his right hand a page holding a flat silver cross with engravings on it. The general effect, Alvarez thought, was very like the pictures of God the Father that the Ethiopians painted on the walls of their churches.

The meeting with the Negus was the high point of Da Lima's embassy. The ruler of Ethiopia, it turned out, wanted the Portuguese army to sweep the Moslems from the Red Sea. Alvarez was asked to draft the details of a formal treaty, though he had to weed out the bizarre notion that the two kings should land sufficient Portuguese and Ethiopians in Arabia to form a line long enough so that they could pass the stones of Mecca from hand to hand and throw them into the sea. Several times Alvarez was called to the imperial tent to explain difficult points to the Negus. On one occasion he found the Negus puzzling over his new map of the world, given to him by Da Lima, and was asked to show exactly where Portugal was located in relation to Ethiopia. Alvarez temporized by claiming that the whole of Portugal was Lisbon, and that all of Spain was Seville. Shrewdly, the half-deceived Negus immediately retorted that it looked from the map as if France should join with Spain and Portugal to make him a larger and more powerful ally.

Everything that Alvarez found so astonishing in the Ethiopians—their violence, the strange ceremonies, their pride and greed—was reflected in the Portuguese themselves. A tiny band of foreigners isolated in the heart of a strange country, the Portuguese behaved like spoiled children. They quarreled incessantly among themselves, with Da Lima and D'Abreu in particular arguing over matters of precedence and causing great embarrassment to the Ethiopians by taking their complaints to the emperor's chamberlain for adjudication. Da Lima complained that D'Abreu was wearing clothes that were too grand for his station and that he was disrespectful; he even claimed that his lieutenant was trying to poison him. Matters finally reached such a pitch that the Portuguese split into two factions, and one day Alvarez had to

The trio of patriarchs opposite, magnificent in their striped turbans, are part of a fresco in the church of Guh, which was probably decorated in the sixteenth or seventeenth century.

rush into the Portuguese tent, swinging his crozier, to break up a bitter sword fight that had begun between Da Lima and D'Abreu.

In the end this quarrel proved to be the Portuguese' undoing. The Negus sent them back to the coast to be picked up at Massawa by a Portuguese squadron, but on the journey tempers flared so high that D'Abreu's faction tried to ambush and capture its rivals. One of the Portuguese was shot in the leg; there was an unseemly brawl in a village where the party was billeted; and the horrified Ethiopian escort promptly marched the entire embassy back to court for the Negus's judgment. There, they were obliged to spend another five years, moping like unwanted guests on the outskirts of the Negus's camp.

Only Alvarez used the long delay wisely. He turned tourist and wandered about the countryside viewing its wonders. He went to see the astonishing churches of Lalibela, measured the towering stone columns of Axum, which he believed were left there by King Solomon, and went hunting for the treasure of the Queen of Sheba. For a while he seriously considered staying on in the country and joining an Ethiopian monastery. By the spring of 1526, when the embassy finally got away, he had enough material to fill five lengthy parts of his description of a slightly tarnished kingdom of Prester John.

But two years later, about the time Alvarez's book came out in Europe, the Portuguese, having found the long-sought king of the eastern Christians, learned that they would have to go to his rescue. For Ethiopia suffered the most calamitous invasion of her history. Striking from the north, Ahmad ibn Ibrahim El Ghazi, commonly called El Gran, "the left-handed," overran the country with an army that included Turkish musketeers and janissaries. His troops ravaged the country, burning villages and selling the inhabitants into slavery. The splendid church decorations that Alvarez had so admired were hacked to shreds; one of the Negus's sons was killed and another sent to be a

One of Ethiopia's many clerics, the priest above carries his ensign—a cross of silver.

pasha's slave in Arabia. The royal treasury was looted. A thousand years of Ethiopian culture collapsed beneath the onslaught. Finally, the Negus himself died like a hunted jackal on the shore of Lake Tana, leaving the crown to his seventeen-year-old heir, Galawedos. Desperate appeals were smuggled out to the Portuguese in India, but it seemed that the rising tide of Islam, drawn by the crescent moon of Turkey, was about to engulf the last outpost of Christian Africa.

The champion whom Portugal sent to Prester John was Dom Christoval da Gama, and he was, fittingly, the quintessential knight-errant—young, gifted, and chivalrous. His father, the illustrious Vasco da Gama, had led the first Portuguese fleet to reach India, and his brother Estevam was the reigning viceroy of India. It was Estevam who arranged for a relief fleet to sail to Ethiopia's aid with as many soldiers as he could spare. Dom Christoval's task was to put fresh heart into the Negus's defense while Portugal raised a proper army to come to his assistance. In the summer of 1541, he and a small expeditionary force were put ashore at Massawa by a Portuguese battle squadron. He was not yet twenty-six.

Cautiously, Da Gama struck inland. His eighteen-month effort to link up

with Galawedos is a story of extraordinary courage and perseverance against overwhelming odds. More than once he managed to elude capture by Gran, but in February, 1543, trapped by a vastly superior Turkish army, his little band was set upon and massacred. The Portuguese commander, taken prisoner, was brought before Gran, sitting triumphant beside a mound of one hundred and sixty Portuguese heads. Da Gama was stripped and flogged; his beard was waxed and twisted into wicks that were set alight; and his eyelids were pulled off with tweezers. Then he was decapitated.

Ironically, Da Gama's squalid death was Galawedos's salvation. Gran, confident that he had crushed his enemy, allowed his Turkish troops to disperse and retired to the area of Lake Tana. There he was surprised by a large army under Galawedos surging out of the hills and accompanied by the surviving Portuguese. Da Gama was avenged when a Portuguese musketeer shot and killed Gran.

His death was the high-water mark of the Moslem invasion, and it was also the beginning of a new relationship between Portugal and Ethiopia. The remnant of Da Gama's tiny army was handsomely treated. The Negus offered them lands, high-born Ethiopian wives, and titles; and many decided to stay. In their wake came Portuguese priests to argue Coptic theology, and Portuguese architects to design castles and palaces at the Negus's command.

Portuguese art and technology were to influence Ethiopian thought and literature for the next hundred years, and for a while the Negus himself acknowledged the authority of the pope, until a nationalist revolt expelled the foreigners and their doctrines. Portugal's adventure in Ethiopia died, as it had begun, in an aura of bloodshed and martyrdom that finally quenched the dream of Prester John.

Timothy Severin's article is taken from his next book, The African Adventure, *to be published this fall by E. P. Dutton.*

Two Ethiopian choirboys mark Palm Sunday by wearing crosses of grass. To Ethiopians the cross is not only a symbol of faith but of their national resistance to the once mighty tides of Islam.

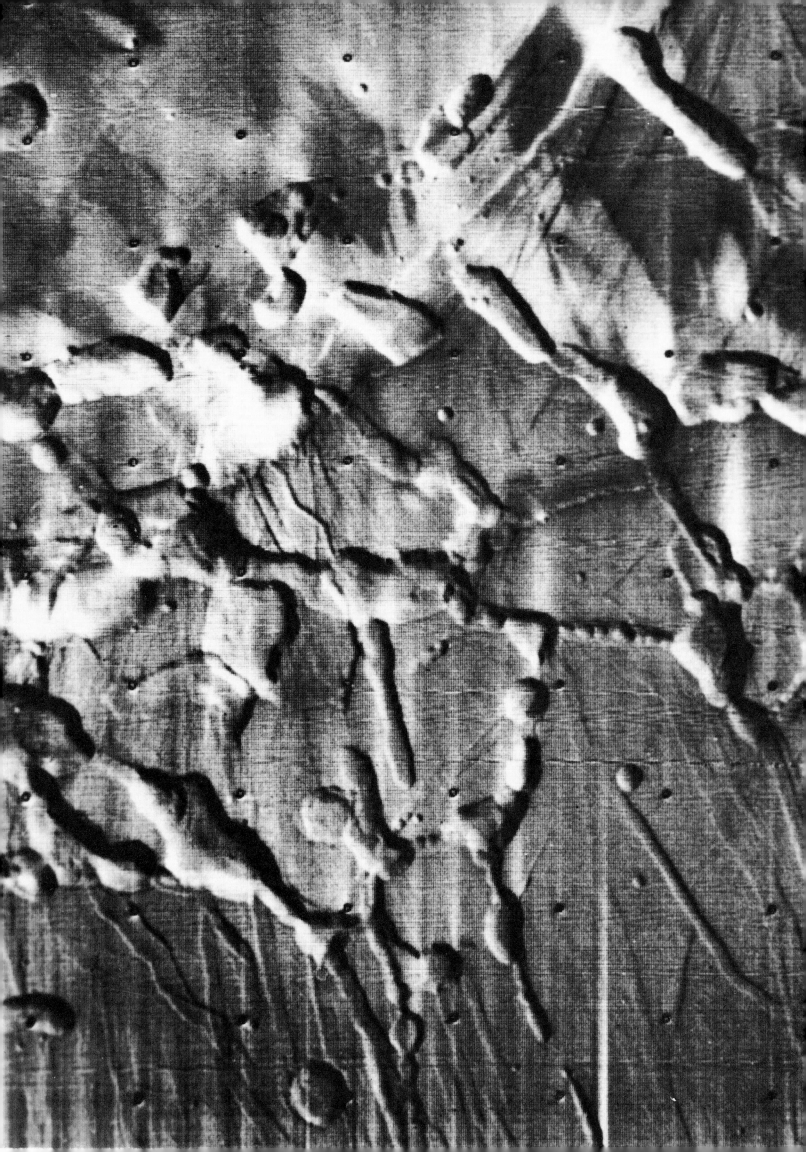

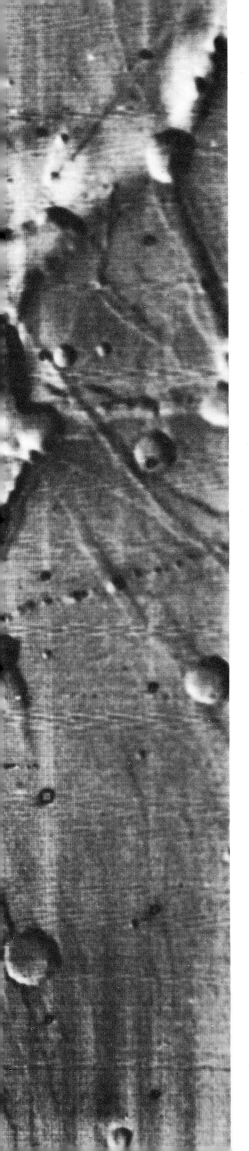

OF MARS MARTIANS AND MARINER 9

Does life lie hiding in the caves
and ice caps of today's Mars, waiting for a more
hospitable climate to return?

By CARL SAGAN

"Now they say there is water on Mars!"

*The weathered face of Mars: in the Mariner 9 photograph at left, covering
an area about 300 miles wide and the same distance high, narrow trenches—
which may have been produced by wind erosion—look like blisters in the
low-angle sunlight streaming in from upper right. The pockmarks are impact
craters. Mars appears to be dry, yet it does contain water—in the polar caps,
in rocks, and in permafrost—though not,* pace *Alan Dunn, in open pools.*

I first became aware that Mars was a place of some interest by reading stories by Edgar Rice Burroughs, who is also known for his invention of Tarzan. Burroughs created a gentleman adventurer from Virginia named John Carter, who was able to transport himself to the planet Mars by standing in an open field and spreading his arms out and wishing. At an early age I tried very hard to test the Carter method. But no matter how hard I tried, I failed, although I always thought there might be a chance.

The Mars that Burroughs imagined was called Barsoom. In fact, he used a lovely phrase, "the hurtling moons of Barsoom," which are the two moons of Mars, Phobos and Deimos. Barsoom was a dying planet, with drying canals and races of ancient peoples. But where did these ideas come from?

Classically, the first impetus for the concept of a dying Mars derives from the nebular hypothesis of Kant and Laplace, a view of the origin of the solar system not too different from what is fashionable today. A vast gas and dust cloud of interstellar dimensions contracts, and spins up as it does so to conserve angular momentum. As escape velocity is reached in the equatorial plane, little blobs of matter are spun off progressively in the outer regions of the solar system, each of which condenses into a planet. This meant that the outermost planets, like Mars, were older and the innermost ones, like Venus, were younger. If you believed that the time interval of formation was significant compared to the age of the solar system, Mars might be a great deal older, Venus a great deal younger, than the Earth. Thus Mars could be imagined as a dying Earth and Venus as the Earth hundreds of millions of years ago. Today we know that the time interval for the formation of the planets was very short compared with the lifetime of the solar system, and so that kind of age difference cannot be of very much significance.

The observational basis for the idea of Mars as a dying world was provided

first by the Italian astronomer Giovanni Schiaparelli, but was publicized consummately by an American Brahmin from Boston named Percival Lowell, a diplomat to Korea turned astronomer. Lowell advocated observing Mars from a place where the atmosphere is reasonably steady (or, as the astronomer says, where the "seeing" is good). Then by eyeball astronomy you look through the telescope and draw pictures of what you see. Lowell was, unfortunately, one of the worst draftsmen who ever sat down at a telescope, and the Mars he drew was composed of little polygonal blocks connected by a multitude of straight lines. These were the straight lines that had first been reported by Schiaparelli in 1877. He called these lines *canali*, which in Italian means channels or grooves. But it was translated as canals, and the whole hypothesis was stated in the translation. Fundamentally, Lowell's argument was that no natural process could produce such a network of long straight lines; hence, they were artificial; hence, there were artisans on Mars.

Some of the flavor of the debate on the canals appears in a few sentences from Lowell. Even then, astronomers knew that Mars had much less water than the Earth does. Lowell says, "The fundamental fact of the matter is the dearth of water. If we keep this in mind we shall see that many of the objections that spontaneously arise answer themselves. The supposed herculean task of constructing such canals disappears at once; for, if the canals could be dug for irrigation purposes, it is evident that what we see, and call by ellipsis the canal, is not really the canal at all, but the strip of fertilized land bordering it —the thread of water in the midst of it, the canal itself, being far too small to be perceptible. In the case of an irrigation canal seen at a distance, it is always the strip of verdure, not the canal, that is visible, as we see in looking from afar upon irrigated country on the Earth." This is in response to one of the major objections to the idea of canals, namely, that they would be too small to see.

The basic idea was that there were canals constructed by a race of vast intelligence on the planet to channel the waters from the melting polar caps to the thirsty inhabitants of the equatorial cities. This brings up two questions: Are there such features on Mars? And, if they are present on Mars, need it be for the reasons that Lowell imagined?

Let us turn to other planetary astronomers. The first statement is by E. E. Barnard in 1894: "I have been watching and drawing the surface of Mars. It is wonderfully full of detail. There is certainly no question about there being mountains and large, greatly elevated, plateaus. To save my soul, I can't believe in canals as Schiaparelli [or Lowell] draws them. I see details where he has drawn none. I see details where some of his canals are, but they are not straight lines *at all*. . . . I verily believe, for all the verifications, that the canals as depicted by Schiaparelli are a fallacy and that they will be proved so before many favorable oppositions are past."

And a second skeptical remark made by E. M. Antoniadi: "At the first glance in the $32\frac{3}{4}$ inch [telescope] on September 20, 1909, I thought I was dreaming and scanning Mars from his outer satellite. The planet revealed a prodigious and bewildering amount of sharp or diffused natural, irregular detail, all held steadily; and it was at once obvious that the geometrical network of single and double canals discovered by Schiaparelli was a gross illusion. Such detail could not be drawn; hence, only its coarser markings were recorded in the notebook."

The latter two descriptions conform closely with what we now know of the appearance of Mars. The canals of Mars are probably due to the eye's penchant for order. It is much simpler to draw disconnected fine details as a few lines, joining them up, than to put down all the irregular mottlings observed in an instant of good seeing. There is no question that the straightness of the lines is due to intelligence. The only question concerns which side of the telescope the intelligence is on.

Matthias Hirzgarter, a seventeenth-century Swiss mathematician, drew Mars as a three-sided rock, bearing the planet's traditional symbol, from data supplied by an Italian astronomer, Francesco Fontana. Of the Mars portraits below, the first two were done in 1659 and 1666; the third, drawn in 1877 by Giovanni Schiaparelli, reveals the straight lines he called canali. *Fired by this "discovery," the American Percival Lowell conceived of Mars as a vast irrigation project and drew the map of its towns and waterways at right. But these canals existed only in the eye of the beholder, and not on Mars.*

LOWELL OBSERVATORY, FLAGSTAFF, ARIZONA; BELOW, LEFT AND RIGHT: SAME; CENTER: W. LEY AND W. VON BRAUN, *The Exploration of Mars,* LONDON, 1956

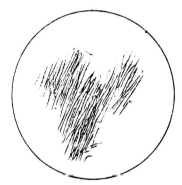

Mars by Christian Huygens

. . . Jean Dominique Cassini

. . . and Giovanni Schiaparelli

Lowell appreciated this perfectly well: "The straightness of the lines is unhesitatingly attributed to the draughtsman." Now, he says, this is a very telling point, "for it is a case of the double-edged sword. Accusation of design, if it proves not to be due to the draughtsman, devolves *ipso facto* upon the canals."

This is the highest level of the pro-canal polemic. There are other levels. In a book called *World Making,* published in 1898, Samuel Phelps Leland says, "When next the planet and the Earth come in opposition great discoveries will then be made. The planet will be high in the heavens. The telescope of the Chicago University with its 40″ glass will probably then be completed. The telescope will almost double the space penetrating power of the 36″ refractor at Mt. Hamilton" (a slight mathematical error, since $40^2/36^2$ does not equal 2). Then comes the terrific part: "With such a power it will be possible to see cities on Mars, to detect navies in its harbors and the smoke of great manufacturing cities and towns. And it may be possible to flash electrical signals across the space which could be readily seen by the inhabitants of Mars with telescopes of considerable power and the answer easily seen by us." According to Leland, there can be "little doubt" that Mars is inhabited. "His [that is, Mars's] conditions are all favorable for life and life of a high order. It is not improbable that there are beings there with a civilization as high if not higher than our own." And then he concludes, "Is it possible to know this of a certainty? Certainly."

The scientific discussions on Mars during this period were obviously not always at the highest intellectual level, but surely the idea of life on Mars was very exciting. There was one man who looked at it from the vantage point not of the professional astronomer, not of the professional publicist, and not of the science-fiction writer. This man was

Alfred Russel Wallace, who was the co-discoverer, with Charles Darwin, of evolution by natural selection and a very clever fellow. Asked to review a book of Lowell's, his criticism, written in a white heat, was itself of book length, and was published in 1906 as *Is Mars Habitable?* Wallace attacked Lowell on physical, not biological grounds. He discovered an error in Lowell's estimate of the albedo of the Earth (the fraction of incident sunlight reflected by a surface) and correctly deduced a mean temperature of Mars of about 230° K, well below the freezing point of water, which is 273° K on the absolute, or Kelvin, scale. Lowell thought that Mars had a temperature comparable to the south of England, apparently the temperature standard of the time. Wallace believed that the annual temperature variation was extreme, that the polar ice caps were at least in part made of condensed carbon dioxide, that the surface material was porous, that craters were present in abundance on the planet's surface, that large amounts of water vapor were not to be found because of gravitational escape, that the canals, if they existed, were related to geologic faults, and that Phobos and Deimos were residua of the formation of the planet. He was at this point just on the verge of deducing subsurface permafrost on the planet. However, the book was not published until Wallace was eighty-three, and he died shortly thereafter.

Reading Wallace's book, I am astounded by the excellence of his logical powers and the currency of many of his conclusions. He had occasional lapses, such as his conclusion that Mars is more like the moon than the Earth. Also, the fact that he thought there was no water at all led him to conclude, "Mars not only is not inhabited by in-

In 1908 H. G. Wells fancifully described "The Things that Live on Mars" for Cosmopolitan. *"There are certain features," he wrote in the passage that accompanied the illustration above, "in which they are likely to resemble us. And as likely as not they will be covered with feathers or fur. It is no less reasonable to suppose, instead of a hand, a group of tentacles or proboscis-like organs."*

telligent beings as Mr. Lowell postulates but is absolutely UNINHABITABLE" (i.e., by large organisms).

After Wallace, the debate passed from scientific works through Sunday supplements to science-fiction writers' minds, and then spread to a vast public to establish the popular views of what Mars was like. Slowly, more information was acquired about Mars, with the development of new optical and radio telescopes on the surface of the Earth, and then with the first flyby spacecraft, Mariners 4, 6, and 7, which briefly glimpsed the planet's surface as they passed it on their orbits around the sun.

Yet, on the eve of the injection of Mariner 9 into Mars orbit in November, 1971, our knowledge of Mars was still characterized by poor data, wish-

ful thinking, overcautious conservatism, a strange kind of Earth-moon parochialism, and too sweeping generalizations from a few good facts. After the end of the Mariner 9 mission, all this changed, and the study of Mars altered from a data-poor, theory-rich situation to a data-rich, theory-poor one. We are now inundated with hard facts. The television cameras alone obtained more than 7,200 photographs of the planet, mapping the entire surface to a resolution of 1 kilometer, and a small percentage of the surface to a resolution of about 100 meters. We have thousands of spectra—ultraviolet spectra giving information on the surface topography, atmospheric aerosols and composition, and the temperature of the upper atmosphere from which leakage of molecules to space occurs; and infrared spectra providing data on surface topography and composition, atmospheric structure and winds, and minor constituents. The surface has been peppered with infrared radiometer examinations of the temperature variation through the day, yielding insights into the thermal properties and porosity of the surface. More than a hundred places on Mars have been examined by the S-band occultation experiment, giving the structure of the atmosphere and ionosphere above these places and the distance of these places from the center of Mars. And the celestial mechanics experiment has begun to map the distribution of mass in the planet's interior.

The Mars revealed by Mariner 9 does not correspond to comprehensive views of the planet imagined earlier. There are certainly no canals as Schiaparelli or Lowell drew them. And, as I expected, Mariner 9 has examined a sufficient area of Mars at a high enough resolution to exclude the presence of a civilization of terrestrial extent and level of development. The planet-wide feudal-technological civilization envisioned by Edgar Rice Burroughs does not exist.

But neither is Mars like the moon. There are cratered terrains, it is true; but there are also large regions on Mars breathtakingly different from our natural satellite. Enormous volcanoes rise ten to twenty miles above their surroundings. Apart from the polar caps, they were the first features seen on the planet when Mariner 9 went into orbit around Mars, despite a severe dust storm. The peaks of the volcanoes were sticking up through the dust. As the storm cleared we gradually obtained better views of their flanks and calderas.

The biggest of these volcanoes, Nix Olympica, is larger than the largest such construct—the Hawaiian Islands—on the planet Earth. The flanks of these volcanoes are remarkably free of impact cratering, implying that they were produced in geologically recent times, perhaps only in the last tens or few hundreds of millions of years. This means that Mars is geologically active on a colossal scale. Besides the huge volcanoes, there are arrays of linear features—not like canals, generally not in the positions of the old canals, and normally not visible from Earth, but nevertheless more or less linear gouges, stretch marks on the skin of Mars. The greatest of these, the enormous Coprates rift valley, runs east-west for 80 degrees of Martian longitude and is comparable in extent to the great East African rift-valley system, the largest on the planet Earth. We do not know if the Coprates rift valley was produced, as the East African rift valley was, by continental drift, a sign of convection in the interior of the planet and of great geologic activity. But whatever the origin of these gouges, they do speak well for a geologically vigorous Mars.

As the dust storm on Mars cleared, I was astonished and delighted to see, laid down on the Martian surface for our edification and appreciation, a set of natural weather vanes and anemometers. Thousands of Martian craters have bright or dark tails of streamlined

shape neatly emanating from them. In a given region most of these tails are parallel. We think many are caused by dust trapped in the crater during the dust storm, and then blown out by a prevailing wind in the final stages of the storm. They need correspond only to a thin veneer of dust—brighter or darker than the surroundings and perhaps a few millimeters thick—but they trace for us the directions of the high winds.

In the Martian tropical zone these crater tails show a clear tendency to follow the prevailing winds on Mars, calculated from meteorological theory and measured by the infrared spec-

Thirty years after H. G. Wells titillated magazine readers with his talk of feathery or furry Martians (see opposite), his near-namesake Orson Welles, above, terrified millions of radio listeners with a fake newscast of an invasion of northern New Jersey by creatures from Mars—who landed in a "huge flaming object" and headed for nearby New York City. Not coincidentally, the program was broadcast on Halloween—October 31, 1938. As people who tuned in late failed to realize, it was a dramatization by the twenty-three-year-old Welles of that rather shopworn thriller *The War of the Worlds* —by none other than H. G. Wells himself. As the show continued, men and women across America panicked; around the site of the putative landing, roads were jammed by refugees fleeing the lethal gas of the Martian invaders. In an hour it was all over, but the impact was so great that few people then alive have forgotten it.

trometer on Mariner 9. At higher latitudes the winds due to the general circulation of Mars—produced by the unequal heating of equator and pole—are predicted to be weak. Therefore, the streaks in these regions are caused by other sorts of winds: winds driven by the enormous elevation differences on Mars; winds like those in the dust devils of the American Southwest; and, near the polar cap, winds driven by the great temperature difference in summer between adjacent frosted and unfrosted terrain. In some places the wind streaks show several directions, probably corresponding to several different occurrences of high-velocity winds.

One striking result of Mariner 9's findings was the discovery that the outline of dark streaks on the Martian surface corresponds quite closely to the outlines of the dark markings viewed by a century of ground-based observations. What is more, the locales of Mars known by Earth-based observations to vary regularly or erratically with the seasons correspond to the areas of Mars in which changes are observed in the constituent wind-blown streaks.

The seasonal changes on Mars have been attributed, at least since the time of Lowell, to vegetation responding to the warmth and wetness of the Martian spring. Lowell even suggested that we were seeing cultivated crops in these annual contrast changes. A few years before Mariner 9, I proposed, in collaboration with Dr. James B. Pollack, that these changes were due to variations in the patterns of wind-blown dust, deposited and lifted by the seasonally varying high-speed winds on Mars. The Mariner 9 observations seem to confirm this view. Thus it appears the seasonal changes are due to meteorology rather than to biology. Yet, there is nothing in these observations that excludes biology, and indeed, at times of great dust storms, ultraviolet light at the surface is significantly attenuated and microorganisms could be rapidly dispersed over the whole of the planet.

There are other clear signs of wind-blown dust on Mars. Mariner 9 found that the insides of many craters have a dark patch or splotch. This splotch frequently appears on the interior part of a crater corresponding to the direction from which the streaks from this or adjacent craters emanate. The dark splotches and bright streaks are most probably produced by winds deflating light-colored particles from the interior, thus revealing the underlying dark material, and then depositing these particles outside the crater and downwind.

These splotches require transporting only thin layers of dust, but other splotches are revealed as enormous sand-dune fields. The best developed of these bears a remarkable similarity to the Great Sand Dunes National Monument in Colorado. Here we see clear evidence of the long-term effects of prevailing winds on mobile particulate matter. By photographing the same region successively throughout the mission, we uncovered many dark streaks and splotches that were slowly increasing in size. Thus we saw the dust transportation in progress.

Because the Martian atmosphere is so thin, higher winds are necessary to make dust particles move. I believe that in the middle of the Mars atmosphere the minimum wind speed necessary to make a sand grain roll over on the surface is 50 to 70 meters per second (110 to 150 miles per hour), compared with only a few meters per second for sand-grain movement on the Earth. Therefore, the erosion and abrasion due to wind-blown sand on Mars must be very great. In areas of strong prevailing winds the erosion rate may be as high as a tenth of an inch to an inch per year. The high winds and mobile dust, in addition to causing the bright and dark markings and the seasonal changes, pose a significant hazard for space vehicles landing on Mars. Indeed, it is not unlikely that the failure of the Soviet Mars 3 entry probe in December, 1971, was caused in part by the high winds during a dust storm.

Perhaps the least expected finding from Mariner 9 is that Mars appears to be covered with a great variety of irreg-

ular channels—some of which have meanders and tributaries (and tributaries of tributaries) and do not start or end in a crater. These sinuous channels are strongly concentrated near the Martian equator, a fact pointing directly to the conclusion that the channels depend on temperatures higher than normal for Mars. They must have been carved out by a liquid flowing steadily on the Martian surface. If this liquid is to be made of not exceptionally exotic stuff, and if it requires high Martian temperatures for its flow, it can only be water. But water cannot exist on Mars—or at least the Mars we see today. The total pressure is not great enough to keep water liquid for an extensive period of time. I am therefore led to the conclusion that these channels were gouged out at a time when the Martian environment was significantly different from what it is today—a time of higher pressure, temperature, and water abundance. Because of the freshness of the channels this epoch could not have been in the earliest stages of Martian history.

From the ultraviolet spectrometer experiment on Mariner 9 we know that substantial quantities of water could not have escaped from Mars, even in the entire course of its existence. Therefore, if the channels are truly river basins, the water that carved them and the dense atmosphere that kept that water liquid must still exist somewhere on the planet today. We know that the minerals in much of the Martian surface contain a great deal of chemically bound water, i.e., water of crystallization. In fact, about one per cent of the Martian surface material is composed of such water. This is the equivalent of an enormous reservoir, and, if Martian organisms do exist, they may find the deserts of Mars more like oceans. And there is undoubtedly subsurface permafrost—water ice frozen at low temperatures beneath the Martian surface.

But the great repositories of volatile gases on Mars are the polar caps. Mariner 9 has now confirmed my earlier guess that the total thickness of the per-

manent polar caps of Mars is about a mile. If all this frost were somehow converted into gas, it would result in a total pressure over the Martian surface of about 1 atmosphere, which is approximately the same as the surface pressure on the Earth today. What is more, the close-up photographs of the permanent polar caps show bright and dark bandings, or laminae, possibly caused by alternating epochs depositing ice and dust, dust and ice. Thus both the channels and the laminae point to a major variation in the Martian climate.

We are actively exploring how such a variation could occur. Alterations in the output of light from the sun, or changes in the tilt of the Martian axis of rotation, could be possible causes of such a phenomenon. But the most straightforward explanation involves changes in the brightness of the polar caps by deposition and removal of dark dust.

The process would be something like this: begin with Mars as it is today, in a vast global ice age, with a large frozen atmosphere at the polar cap. Then assume an epoch in which dark dust is deposited at the polar caps, perhaps by events like the great dust storm during the beginning of the Mariner 9 mission. The atmospheric pressure on Mars is probably due largely to the temperature of the polar caps. These caps are, at least in significant part, composed of solid carbon dioxide, and the total pressure on Mars is just the amount of carbon dioxide gas we would expect to find in equilibrium with solid carbon dioxide (dry ice) at the pole. The general-circulation winds on Mars make hot air at the equator rise, and carry it toward the poles, where it settles. However, the atmosphere is so thin that this hot air plays a very small role in heating the poles. But dust deposited at the poles causes a greater absorption of sunlight there, resulting in a slightly greater atmospheric pressure. The heat transported from equator to pole now goes into warming the polar cap somewhat more efficiently. The atmospheric pressure then becomes even greater; hot air transported from equator to pole is even more efficient in heating the pole; and we have what I call an advective runaway, which continues until all the material in the polar cap is vaporized. As a result of the runaway, the Martian climate moves entrancingly toward a much more Earthlike climate, and it is at these times, I believe, that the Martian channels are carved out by running water near the equator.

The return to conditions similar to those of today occurs with all the factors running the opposite way: a long period of no dust at the poles, with the result that the poles remain bright and absorb less sunlight and thus get colder and cause more frost to be deposited there. The atmospheric pressure then declines, heat transport from equator to pole is less efficient, the pole cools even more, and we reach a situation like the present one.

While I see no significant impediment to there being contemporary biology on Mars, it is obviously easier to imagine biology on Mars at the time of more Earthlike conditions; and it is not out of the question to suppose that there are organisms on Mars in hibernation or some other sort of biological repose, awaiting the end of the Martian ice age.

It is still too early to tell if this view of climatic instability on Mars is the correct one. But it has already produced a set of analyses that may be of great use in understanding ice ages on the Earth and how to avoid them. These findings suggest that the amount of particulates in the atmosphere—for example, from industrial pollution—can have a major effect on the terrestrial climate. Further, because of the present absence of

Is there life on Mars? While scientists debate the question, purveyors of mass entertainment have been busy, as the pictures on this page show, giving the public the Martians it wants—i.e., beings not too unlike themselves. In reality, however, if Mars is inhabited, the Martians will surely be very dissimilar to any earthly organisms, thanks to the randomness of biological evolution.

Martians from darkest Hollywood take wing in the Republic Pictures film In Darkest Africa.

Mars Attacks the World *(1938)*

TV's favorite Martian, Roy Walston

These Invaders from Mars *(1953) are simply doing their thing.*

Buster Crabbe checks evil single-handedly in Universal's serial Flash Gordon's Trip to Mars.

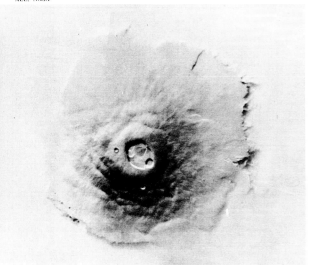

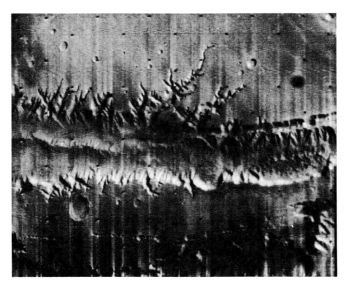

The volcano Nix Olympica, 300 miles across   *A section of the 3,000-mile-long great rift valley, at center*   *A meandering valley probably*

A windswept world: Mariner 9 photographs like the ones found on these pages convey the variety of Mars's topography and provide a great deal of information on the planet's nature. Huge volcanoes rise ten to twenty miles above the surrounding country; the fact that their flanks are for the most part free of impact craters indicates that they are of comparatively recent origin and also that the planet is geologically active. Its rift valleys may have been caused by continental drift. The polar caps of Mars are presumably composed of frozen carbon dioxide—mixed, perhaps, with crystals of ice.

water on Mars, the circulation of the Martian atmosphere seems much simpler than that of the Earth's atmosphere, and a great deal of information about the weather on Earth may be found by studying the weather on Mars.

In *The Sands of Mars* Arthur C. Clarke imagined a long-term biological reconditioning of Mars—making it more habitable for human beings by the appropriate breeding of plants from Earth. The foregoing ideas on climatic variation on Mars suggest that periodically much more Earthlike conditions are naturally brought about, and that by adjusting the amount of dark material at the polar caps, we might hasten the return of more clement conditions. But such human intervention into the Martian environment should be undertaken, if at all, only after a long and comprehensive study of the present physical and biological Martian environment.

I suppose it is just barely possible that

the Mars Lowell and Burroughs wrote about may have existed in the past, or may exist in the future. But I wouldn't bet on it. If there is life on Mars, it will probably be astonishingly unlike any sort of life on Earth—unless we muck up the planet by failing to sterilize our spacecraft, thus introducing hostile terrestrial microorganisms into the environment there, with results we are currently unable to predict.

The data provided by the voyage of Mariner 9 suggest that, at least at some times and in some places, Mars may be much more habitable for terrestrial microorganisms than many had suspected possible. They also show us dramatically that ultraviolet light from the sun (which could fry terrestrial microorganisms in approximately one second) can be prevented from striking the surface by dust in the atmosphere, and that particles the size of microorganisms can be rapidly transported all over the surface of the planet. These factors make it more urgent to insist upon sterilization of spacecraft intended for Mars landings.

The dangers in contamination of Mars are twofold: the possibility of landing organisms that will then be registered on our life detectors—surely an extremely expensive way to investigate common terrestrial microorganisms; and the possibility of doing ecological damage to a Martian biota, if one exists. It is thus rewarding to see, despite the cost of sterilization, the measures that are being taken by the two great space-faring nations.

At a meeting held in Madrid in May, 1972, Professor V. I. Vashkov of the Soviet Ministry of Health outlined in detail the procedures used to sterilize the Mars 2 and 3 entry vehicles—the first Earth spacecraft to land on the surface of Mars. Vashkov told of an elaborate and exceptionally careful procedure, involving heat, gaseous sterilization, and high-energy radiation. The sterilized spacecraft was then wrapped in a shroud filled with gaseous sterilants, and this shroud was not divested until the spacecraft was out of the Earth's atmosphere. The same procedure was used on a dummy spacecraft, which, when carefully analyzed on Earth, showed not a single microorganism in it. The United States Viking program has similarly elaborate plans—involving heat-soaking the spacecraft and subsequently enclosing it in a shroud.

There was one further bonus from Mariner 9—the first close-up photographs of Phobos and Deimos, the Martian satellites that had been thought by some to be artificial satellites launched by an ancient Martian civilization. Instead we find both satellites to be old, dark, battered, and entirely natural objects. This will probably come as a disappointment to certain people, but the two possible explanations of the origins of Phobos and Deimos are almost as interesting as the disproved romantic hypothesis. Either they are captured asteroids, in which case we have had our first close-up look at these elusive in-

carved by running water   The south polar cap, contracted almost to its minimum limits   Laminations near the south polar cap, high land at top left

habitants of our solar system; or, as suggested by Alfred Russel Wallace, they are debris left over from the origin of Mars. We hope, in the near future, to decide between these alternatives.

The Mars revealed by Mariner 9 is one that is meteorologically, geologically, and, just possibly, biologically much more interesting than many scientists had previously suspected. But Mariner 9, despite its enormous quantity of data, has viewed Mars only from a narrow perspective, just as the Earth viewed by Apollo from Earth orbit gives little hint of the existence of hills and streams and trees—to say nothing of mice and microbes. In the same way, Mariner 9 gives little or no information about the close-up character of the Martian surface. Such an exploration requires a landing mission.

The United States has plans under way to land two spacecraft on Mars in the summer of 1976. July 4, 1976, is

a possible, and therefore probably an inevitable, date for the first landing. These Viking spacecraft are remarkably sophisticated combinations of scientific instruments to examine Mars for microorganisms, organic chemistry, surface mineralogy, winds, Marsquakes, magnetic dust, exotic atmospheric gases, and many other phenomena.

The preliminary plans are for the first Viking lander to make Martian landfall in a region called Chryse—the land of gold. It is a place that appears to be low enough so that the Viking aerodynamic braking system will work; smooth enough so that the lander will not tumble over; generally wind-free enough so that it will not be blown over; and soft enough so that there will be material for the automated scoop to pick up. By great good fortune, it is also scientifically interesting, for Chryse is a region of sinuous tributaried channels—the presumptive relics of a past epoch of

running water and clement conditions on Mars. We are thus on the doorstep of another epic phase in our exploration of Mars. No one knows what the Viking landers will uncover, but if Mariner 9 is any guide, astonishments, delights, and high scientific adventure are probable.

Mars and its moons are only a small sampling of the nine planets, thirty-two moons, and innumerable asteroids and comets that fill our solar system. There is our nearest planetary neighbor, Venus, a hellhole of a world, which may, however, offer a cautionary tale for the evolution of the Earth. There is Mercury, a place of very high density, which may be a world with its crust and upper mantle stripped off in the early history of the solar system. Beyond Mars are the Jovian planets, which dominate our solar system as seen from afar. Almost all the mass and angular momentum of the solar system reside in Jupiter, Saturn, Uranus, and Neptune. These giant planets have retained the hydrogen-rich gases of the early solar system—the gases from which life on Earth evolved. And the comets may be the most pristine samples available to us of the material that formed the solar system. They are also basically interstellar objects, spending most of their lifetimes in the dark between the stars.

Within this vast array of worlds in our solar system—which we already know to be a fascinating collection—there are bound to be surprises. One recently emerging surprise is Titan, the largest satellite of Saturn and a world

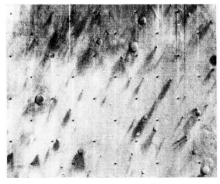

In the crater field seen at left, almost every crater is accompanied by a dark streak parallel to its neighbors. Streaks of this nature are probably formed by dark dust that is trapped in the craters by storms and then blown out by high-velocity prevailing winds. At right, the set of bright streaks in the high Tharsis plateau is made up of wind-blown sand or dust, but just how the streaks are produced is not yet understood.

about the size of the planet Mercury. Recent work shows that Titan has a dense atmosphere, brilliant red clouds, and a surface temperature much higher than it should have for its great distance from the sun. Titan is about ten times farther from the sun than the Earth is and receives about 1/100 of the sunlight. But its surface seems to be almost twice as hot as an object that far from the sun should be. The explanation seems to be the greenhouse effect, which shuts in the thermal infrared radiation given off by the surface of Titan. The molecule responsible for the Titanium greenhouse effect appears to be molecular hydrogen, the most abundant molecule in the universe. The surface atmospheric pressure may be a few tenths of that on Earth (Titan has a much denser atmosphere than Mars does today), but the gravity of Titan is weak enough to allow the hydrogen to escape rapidly into interplanetary space. The density of the solid body of Titan is low, approximately 2 grams per cubic centimeter—about halfway between rock and water—and the interior is probably composed of snows and ices of water, methane, and ammonia, the same ices thought to compose the comets.

What is happening on the surface of Titan seems to be this: the snows of the interior are melted by radioactive heat, and gush to the surface through cracks and fumaroles and perhaps volcanoes of methane, ammonia, and water. These gases, upon reaching the atmosphere of Titan, are broken apart by ultraviolet sunlight. One product of their ultraviolet irradiation is hydrogen, which heats the surface through the greenhouse effect before it escapes into space. But, as we know from laboratory experiments with such gases, there are other products—complex organic molecules, many of which are brownish-red. Thus the color of Titan's clouds may indicate the large-scale presence

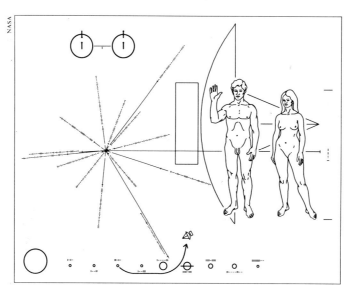

Author Carl Sagan's ingenious "message," above, about its senders was launched last year on a plaque on Pioneer 10, the first spacecraft to leave the solar system. Even if it chances to reach some distant civilization, will its recipients be able to "read" it?

of complex organic molecules there.

The Jovian planets probably are similarly loaded with organic compounds, and the entire outer solar system may be a great natural laboratory working on the chemistry of the origin of life for the past 5 billion years. But the gravities on Jupiter, Saturn, Uranus, and Neptune are so high as to make very close approaches or landings on them impractical, at least in the near future. Titan, however, is a much more accessible object, and will probably be the first object rich in such organic matter to be investigated. The two projected Mariner Jupiter/Saturn flybys of 1977 will arrive near Jupiter in 1979 and Saturn in 1981. The targeting of such space vehicles is now sufficiently in hand so that a craft could fly within a few hundred miles of Titan, to examine the brilliant red clouds, the atmospheric composition, and the as yet unseen surface by instruments of the sort proved out by Mariner 9.

But, like the Viking project, Mariner Jupiter/Saturn is in financial trouble, although it would cost about the same as did the American aircraft shot down in Vietnam during Christmas week of 1972. I find that comparison particularly poignant: life vs. death, hope vs. fear. Space exploration and the highly mechanized destruction of people use similar technology, some of the same

manufacturers, and similar human qualities of organization and daring. Can we not hope that with the Vietnam cease-fire we can now make the transition from automated killing to automated exploration of our solar system?

The advantages of such exploration are varied and compelling. I believe the scientific perspective obtained by observing neighboring worlds in the solar system will have practical benefits here on Earth, apart from the sense of peaceful adventure and the exhilaration of exploration, coming at a time when all the Earth's surface has been explored. When our sciences of meteorology, geology, and biology are generalized by contact with other examples elsewhere, their powers will be vastly enhanced. Space exploration also gives us a new perspective on our planet, its origins and its possible futures. We see the Earth as it is, one planet among many, a world whose significance is only what we make it. We realize that if there is life elsewhere, it almost certainly will be different from life on Earth, and this makes the similarities among men awesome, compared to their differences.

There is a great need for social reform on Earth, for the eradication of poverty, starvation, and injustice. But in addition to food for the body, we need food for the mind and spirit. As I read human history I find a remarkable correlation between epochs of exploration and discovery and epochs of major cultural advances. By the exploration of the solar system we find out, and make better, who we are.

Carl Sagan, director of Cornell's Laboratory for Planetary Studies, was one of the team that monitored Mariner 9. This article is taken from Mars and the Mind of Man, *by Ray Bradbury, Arthur C. Clark, Bruce Murray, Carl Sagan, and Walter Sullivan, to be published this summer by Harper & Row.*

Opposite: Saturn and its rings. The continuing search for extraterrestrial life now takes in, among other places, this planet's odd satellite, Titan.

A Visit with the Mole and the Eagle

History has cast up many notable duos: Anthony and Cleopatra, for instance, Elizabeth and Essex, Batman and Robin—but none, perhaps, as amiably eccentric as the Webbs, Sidney and Beatrice

In 1927 Malcolm Muggeridge, the noted English journalist and commentator, married Katherine (Kitty) Dobbs, thereby also acquiring a large number of new relatives. Among these was Kitty's indomitable Aunt Beatrice, the wife of Sidney Webb. Together and singly, from the 1880's to the 1940's, the Webbs worked tirelessly for the Socialist cause, helping organize the Fabian Society, publishing numerous tomes, and gathering an illustrious salon about them at Passfield Corner, where, by the 1920's, they had become almost as well known for their eccentricities as for their philosophy. This account of Muggeridge's introduction to the Webbs is taken from *Chronicles of Wasted Time: The Green Stick*, the first volume of his autobiography, which will be published in the United States later this year by William Morrow.

In meeting Kitty's distinguished relatives, for me the big occasion, of course, was going to spend a weekend with the Webbs. I had heard them spoken of in tones of reverence by my father and his friends from my earliest years. So I approached the house they lived in at Passfield Corner with a decided feeling of awe, riding in an ancient hired car that had met us at Liphook Station. The Webbs never had a motorcar of their own. A Scottish maid—one of a pair who served Mrs. Webb for many years—let us in. They were women of the utmost discretion who remained completely unaffected and uncontaminated by the procession of cranks, crackpots, and egomaniacs who flowed through the house; in some mysterious way, they kept to the very end their Scottish self-containment and impregnable complacency. One of them asked Kitty, after we had returned from the U.S.S.R., whether the Five-Year Plan answered. It was a question that indicated, I thought, a very creditable skepticism in spite of the concerted insistence of their employers and most of their guests that the success of every Soviet venture must be assured.

Mrs. Webb was waiting for us in the sitting room, standing, as she so often did, with her back to the fire, and swaying slightly to and fro. She was so completely different from her sister Kate, Lady Courtney: frail and white, almost ghostly, in comparison with

the other's solidity. She rushed at Kitty, hurling herself upon her with a kind of avidity, as though to assure herself that Kitty was indeed there in her bodily presence. I, too, was asked to implant a kiss upon Mrs. Webb's cheek, an experience comparable, I imagine, to kissing the big toe of a marble saint. The thing that struck me about her at once was her beauty, so reminiscent of Kitty's. A beauty of bone rather than of flesh. She was also, as I sensed, tragic; not in any trivial way of deprivation—like losing the lover she fancied (though that had happened, as I learned afterward, in the person, ridiculously enough, of Joseph Chamberlain, a preposterous engraving of a man, with wooden features and a monocle, who habitually wore an orchid in his buttonhole, a Birmingham industrialist and radical turned imperialist). Hers was some deeper tragedy, with which I felt instinctively in sympathy. To do with her restless walks along the Embankment; with her prayers, offered in a silent, cavernous Westminster Abbey, but alas wrongly addressed—dead letters that were never delivered; with sleepless nights and the yearning so often expressed in her journal for the long, definitive sleep of death.

Webb came toddling in. He really was a ridiculous-looking man, with tiny legs and feet, a protruding stomach, and a large head. A sort of pedestrian Toulouse-Lautrec. It was as though Mrs. Webb, not being able to have her monocled giant, chose this dwarf in pince-nez instead. Such temperaments as hers always try to ridicule their own passions by making a moral tale of them, planting gargoyles where the steeple should have climbed into the sky. Webb was her gargoyle, the *reductio ad absurdum* of love and lovers, a Blue Book Abelard or computer Casanova: Sancho Panza to their friend Shaw's Don Quixote. Maybe, I sometimes used to reflect, Shaw would have provided a compromise mate for her, something between the monocle and the pince-nez. She told me once that the first time they were

alone together Shaw "simply threw himself upon me." It was something, she went on, that he did to every woman he met, and she had so sternly rebuffed him that nothing of the kind ever happened again. If the thought had crossed her mind that the tall, red-bearded, pale-faced jester would have been a more diverting companion than the partner she chose, and *Plays, Pleasant and Unpleasant* a more diverting *oeuvre* than the forbidding tomes the Webb partnership produced, about which she always spoke disparagingly, she took a characteristic and terrible revenge by ensuring that Shaw was married, not to one of the luscious actresses like Ellen Terry or advanced ladies like Annie Besant that he occasionally fancied, and she so disliked (she made the word "advanced" somehow more detestable by accentuating the second syllable and shortening the *a*), but to Charlotte Payne-Townshend, an Irish lady of great plainness and considerable wealth. He met her at the Webbs' house; it was Mrs. Webb who made the match and resolutely cut off his retreat when he tried to make a getaway.

Mrs. Webb's household rose early. Before breakfast one would see her, if the weather was fine, roaming about the garden, not with the eye or step of a gardner, but more in the style of a tigress pacing up and down its cage. If she caught sight of one looking out, she would pause and begin a conversation, liable to be even less discreet then than at the indoor sessions. I remember on one such occasion leaning out of the window to hear from her the most scabrous particulars of eminent Labour Party and Fabian Society figures like Ramsay MacDonald and Bertrand Russell and H. G. Wells, most of whom she intensely disliked or despised ("Poor little Wells," she always called him). This side of her nature—curious, gossipy, scandalous—which gives piquancy to her enormous journal, brought out all the true vivacity and charm, the audacity and insolence, in her, so muffled in the partnership with her dreary little consort and their joint

By MALCOLM MUGGERIDGE

enterprises, in which, in my opinion, she had little real interest and played little real part. Certainly, her own writing is quite different in style and mood from their joint efforts.

After lunch Mrs. Webb rested and Sidney was instructed to take a walk with any male visitors who happened to be present; ladies were expected to follow Mrs. Webb's example and lie down—which did not please Kitty. Exercise was considered to be good for Sidney; though his diet was strictly controlled by Mrs. Webb, and certain things, like bacon and eggs, which he particularly appreciated, denied him, he still was a hearty eater and apt to put on weight. Once out of sight of the house, his zest for walking markedly diminished, and he usually looked around for some convenient haystack where he could take a nap. If it was hot and there were flies about, he would knot his handkerchief and wear it on his head. It was on one such occasion that he complained to me that there were no novels of business life that he had been able to discover, and asked whether I knew of any. I mentioned *Dombey and Son* and Upton Sinclair's *The Jungle,* but the suggestions were not acceptable. After a discreet interval, he would shake himself awake, get up, and return to the house, quickening his step so as to arrive in a convincing condition of breathlessness and lather. His physique facilitated this mild deception, since he easily perspired. Mrs. Webb was in the habit of, as it were, issuing brief bulletins about his bodily propensities—"Sidney sweats!" or, explaining the impossibility of their sharing a bedroom, "Sidney snores!"—which he seemed to find inoffensive; even, perhaps, endearing.

The evening was given over to talk, and in Mrs. Webb's case, to an occasional herbal cigarette; in his, a cigar. If there were several guests, Mrs. Webb would arrange them hierarchically. Thus her nephew Stafford Cripps would take precedence over Kitty and me, but we would be given more consideration than some mousy little secretary or archivist allowed to join the company. An earl, actually Bertrand Russell's brother, who had just come into the Labour movement, got better treatment than a don like Harold Laski, who had been in it for years. Sometimes her hierarchical arrangements were enforced at the risk of being thought rude, as in the case of the Dean of Canterbury, Dr. Hewlett Johnson, who turned up after a telephone call inviting himself had given Mrs. Webb the impression it was the archbishop who proposed a visit. The Dean was amiably but firmly put in his place.

All opinions and anecdotes from our hosts were joint ones, delivered with the editorial or royal "we." For instance, describing a visit to Trotsky when he was in exile on the Turkish island of Prinkipo, Mrs. Webb recalled how the one-time Soviet Commissar for War had remarked that even in England a bloody revolution would be required. "We told him *No!*" she triumphantly concluded. While Mrs. Webb regaled us with anecdotes, Sidney sat stroking his beard, with a look of sly contentment on his face, as though just being a party to such glories was enough for him. His little legs seldom reached the ground, and I wondered how it would have been possible for Mrs. Webb's long, lithe body to curl up on so tiny a lap, as she claimed happened when they broke off

The Webbs at Passfield Corner in the 1930's

their labors for a little —her term—"spooning." It seemed an impracticable proposition to me.

By the time the ancient vehicle arrived on Monday morning for the return journey, the Webbs were already at work. I once, with great daring, peeped in at them. He was seated at a desk, as it might have been back at the Colonial Office, where, before his marriage, he worked as a civil servant. A gnomelike amanuensis, pen strokes steady, stance assured. She was prowling about the room as, earlier, she had about the garden. There they were, planning our future, and along lines that actually came to pass in a matter of a very few years. A weird enough pair to be so engaged, to be sure: Beauty and the Beast, twentieth-century style, I thought. Or, better, following Blake, he the mole watching the roots, she the eagle, watching the fruits; he burrowing about the underground, she soaring into some wild

sky of her own imagining. A two-man demolition squad, enormously effective, as it turned out, operating in their snug Hampshire home, with the two Scottish maids keeping everything shipshape, preparing the special scones and shortcake Mrs. Webb found so palatable, and everlastingly asking themselves what, if anything, answered. What the mole got out of it all was obvious; when, as Lord Passfield, he found himself sitting in the Secretary of State's chair in the Colonial Office he felt so contented that, for once, his mind lapsed into total quiescence.

But what of the eagle? What did she hope to get out of it? This was a more complicated question. I got the clue, I think, the last time I saw her, not so very long before she died in 1943. We had been quarreling, more or less publicly, about the Soviet regime, which she had come to adulate and I to detest, thus reversing our positions when we first met. At the same time, she continued to fascinate me, for her beauty, and for that tragic quality in her that she retained to the end, both characteristics that had intensified with age. She, likewise, for some reason, went on wanting to see Kitty and me. So we still visited Passfield occasionally. On this last visit, just as we were leaving, she said she had something to show me. It turned out to be a portrait of Lenin presented to her by the Soviet government, as stylized and cheap, artistically speaking, as any print of a saint of the Church or blessed martyr offered for sale at Lourdes. She had set the picture up as though it were a Velázquez, with special lighting coming up from below and a fine vista for looking at it. It was vivid in its way, showing the tiny eyes, the Mongolian features, the resolute chin and cruel mouth of its subject. For her, I realized, the place was a shrine; she looked positively exalted there —uplifted, worshipful, in an almost frightening way, like someone possessed. A frail, aged bourgeois lady, wearing, as she usually did, a gray silk dress and pretty lace cap on her head, prostrating herself, metaphorically speaking, before the founding father of the twentieth-century totalitarian state, the archterrorist of our time! It was extraordinary and rather horrifying. Afterward, I reflected that the two scenes I had witnessed—the Webbs at work and Mrs. Webb at prayer before her Lenin picture—embodied the whole spirit of the age, showing her to be a true priestess and prophetess, pursuing truth through facts and arriving at fantasy, seeking deliverance through power and arriving at servitude.

CHAPLIN'S

THE GOLD RUSH

"Ridicule," said Chaplin, "is an attitude of defiance: we must laugh in
the face of our helplessness against the forces of nature—or go insane."

With the careers of important artists, in film or elsewhere, there is often agreement as to which work is a man's masterpiece. But with Chaplin, his hottest enthusiasts often disagree in choosing his best film. Some of them deny first place to any of his feature-length works; they prefer his short films. So when one writes about Chaplin in a series on landmark films, one writes about the man, really, not about an obviously "best" picture, and one selects a favorite example to represent him. *The Gold Rush* is a fine work in itself; it is also an emblem of a glorious life's work.

When he made *The Gold Rush* in 1925, Chaplin was thirty-six. He had been a world-famous star for about ten years. Trotsky said of Céline that he "walked into great literature as other men walk into their own homes." The same figure applies to Chaplin and great film. This rising young English music-hall performer met the film medium as it if had been created for him and the film public as if it had been waiting for him. Up to 1920 he made about seventy films, most of them short and most directed by himself. Only one of them, *Tillie's Punctured Romance* (1914), was feature-length, and it was directed by Mack Sennett. In 1921 Chap-

Out to brave and conquer the elements in his city suit, the Lone Prospector clutches a map and surveys the chilly Alaskan snowscape in his 1925 film, The Gold Rush.

lin directed his first feature, *The Kid,* and starred in it with Jackie Coogan. The next feature that he directed, *A Woman of Paris* (1923), was not a comedy; he appeared in it very briefly as a station porter. *The Gold Rush* was only the second long film of his own about the Tramp; yet he knew he was dealing with a character who was familiar to everyone, Eskimos and Malayans included. It's rather as if an author had created a world-renowned character through short stories, had written one successful novel about him, and now wanted to explore that character more deeply in a second long work.

In his autobiography, Chaplin recounts his struggle to find an idea for that second feature, insisting to himself: "This next film must be an epic! The greatest!" Nothing came.

"Then one Sunday morning, while spending the weekend at the Fairbankses', I sat with Douglas after breakfast, looking at stereoscopic views. Some were of Alaska and the Klondike; one a view of the Chilkoot Pass, with a long line of prospectors climbing up over its frozen mountain. . . . Immediately ideas and comedy business began to develop, and, although I had no story, the image of one began to grow."

The role of the unconscious in the creative process is still unfathomed; we can only hypothesize from results. In Chaplin's reaction to those photos, the striking element is unpredictability.

With the exception of *His Prehistoric Past* (1914), a two-reeler, he had never made a film that took the Tramp out of contemporary city or country life. Tramps are, after all, a by-product of modern industry. Evidently, Chaplin's unconscious saw at once the advantages of putting the Tramp into a context that, so to speak, had no direct relation to Trampdom, yet had the possibilities for the "epic" he was seeking. And, presumably, he saw the power of putting the Tramp, whose black mustache is the center of the figure's color graduations, against predominantly white backgrounds. All in all, it was a chance to simultaneously vary and heighten what he had done up to now.

Years later Chaplin told Jean Cocteau that the plot of *The Gold Rush* had grown "like a tree." Well, it is a remarkably ramified tree, a remarkably complex plot for a film that seems simple and runs less than ninety minutes. In brief: Charlie, a prospector in the Alaskan gold rush of 1898, takes refuge from a storm in a lonely, snowbound cabin with another prospector, Big Jim McKay, who had literally been blown there after making a big gold strike. They spend some days of hunger together, then go their separate ways. Big Jim finds a man trying to jump his claim and, in a struggle, is knocked out. He comes to without any memory of his claim's location.

Charlie, meanwhile, has arrived in a

boom town, has found a job as caretaker of a cabin, and has fallen in love with Georgia, a dance-hall girl. Since she is in love with a strapping young prospector, she treats Charlie lightly, until she accidentally discovers how truly smitten the Tramp is. Before Charlie can pursue his love, Big Jim wanders into town, still amnesiac about his claim, and seizes Charlie as the sole means of guiding him back to the lonely cabin near the gold. He promises Charlie half the proceeds and drags him off.

They find the cabin and spend a stormy night there. During the night the cabin is blown to the edge of a cliff near the claim. (This is a reversal of the earlier device in which Big Jim was blown from the claim to the cabin.) In the morning the two prospectors escape from the cabin just before it slips over the cliff edge—to find themselves right on the site of the gold.

In an epilogue, Charlie and Big Jim, swathed in furs, are on board a ship bound for the United States. Charlie puts on his carefully preserved Tramp outfit for newspaper photographers, and runs into Georgia. She thinks he is still just the Tramp, hides him from the ship's officers who are searching for a stowaway, and offers to pay his fare when they find him. The truth is revealed about the new millionaire, and Charlie and Georgia are united.

It *is* the "epic" that Chaplin was looking for. The opening strikes a serious note. The first shots are of a long, serpentine line of prospectors filing up the snow-covered Chilkoot Pass (filmed in Nevada, actually) and are obviously inspired by some of the pictures that Fairbanks showed Chaplin on that Sunday morning. The sequence is grim; we even see one of the prospectors collapse while the others trudge heedlessly past him.

Then a title announces "A Lone Prospector," and we see a narrow mountain path on the edge of a steep drop. I always laugh at once, not just because I know Chaplin is coming and the path is dangerous, but because the scenery—separated from the opening by only one

1.

2.

3.

Hallucinating from hunger, Big Jim (Mack Swain) decides to make a meal out of his companion, but Charlie won't come to dinner. Gun in hand, he prepares to ambush Jim (1), holds him off (2), and, once Jim's delusion has passed, embraces him and forgives all (3).

title—is so patently phony compared with the reality of the pass. Thus, early in the film, Chaplin establishes a contrast that continues throughout: the real world versus the theatre of that world, unblinking reality as the ground for a comic abstract of that reality. It's dangerous to mix modes like that, unless you are able, as Chaplin is, to make each instantly credible and supportive

of the other. Then in he comes, dancing along with a pack on his back.

In his first sequence he shows the touch that made him great. As he skips and skids along the narrow path, a gigantic bear appears behind him and follows him. A lesser comic would have turned, seen the bear, and possibly got a lot of laughs out of panicking on the slippery path. But the bear disappears into a cave just before Charlie turns around. *We* know the danger he has escaped; he doesn't. This is not only funnier, it is also serious: it exemplifies one of the Tramp's qualities—innocence, and an unwitting faith in the power of that innocence.

Later, when he and Big Jim are trapped and starving in the cabin, Big Jim, delirious with hunger, imagines that Charlie is a gigantic chicken. (Big Jim is played by Mack Swain, a fat and endearing figure in early Chaplin films.) The hallucination is funny, but Chaplin says he got the idea from the tragic story of the Donner party, the emigrants who were snowbound in the Sierra Nevadas in the winter of 1846 and resorted to cannibalism. On this odd point Chaplin himself wrote: "In the creation of comedy, it is paradoxical that tragedy stimulates the spirit of ridicule, because ridicule, I suppose, is an attitude of defiance: we must laugh in the face of our helplessness against the forces of nature—or go insane."

From the Donner story, too, he elaborated the famous sequence of the boiled shoe. (Some members of the starving Donner party roasted and ate their moccasins.) Charlie and Big Jim are so famished that they eat a shoe—the Tramp's, of course. Charlie boils and serves it, and the humor comes not only from what they are eating, but from the way they eat it. A lesser comic inventor might have gotten laughs by having the two men grimace in disgust as they forced themselves to chaw. But, as in the bear incident, Chaplin raises the scene to a higher power, making it funnier by means of poetic imagination. Big Jim is jealous because the Tramp has the bigger piece of shoe, and switches plates. This is funnier than grimaces because it is *truer*. Then the Tramp twirls the shoelaces on his fork like spaghetti, sucking each nail as if it were a tasty bone. The consolations of fantasy have rarely gone further.

All through Chaplin's body of work, hunger is a recurrent subject of comedy. (One example among many: in *The Circus* the hungry Tramp steals bites from a child's hot dog over the shoulder of the father who holds the boy in his arms.) Hunger is an inevitable subject for a Tramp, particularly one whose creator grew up in wretched poverty. Three times a day, life puts the Tramp at the mercy of "the forces of nature," and three times a day Chaplin has the option of transmuting those forces into laughter. But there is an extraordinary aspect to this theme in *The Gold Rush*. Usually in Chaplin's films the pinch of hunger comes from a social stringency: no money. Here in the cabin, money is irrelevant. Chaplin takes the theme that has always had a sociopolitical resonance for him, isolates it into the Need Itself, and makes it funnier than ever.

The harmonics of the picture—light tone against dark, light tone arising *out* of dark and vice versa—are enriched by the Tramp's first entrance into the boom-town dance hall. Chaplin, the director, avoids the conventional sequence: showing us the bustling saloon, then showing us the Tramp looking at it—looking at the camera, in fact. He shoots past the Tramp, from behind, to the saloon interior. Charlie is in outline; the brightness is beyond him. He watches from the edge, and we watch from an edge even farther behind him. Yet because we see the Tramp from slightly below eye level, there is something strong—almost heroic—in his pathos, and, simultaneously, there is something comic in his silhouette. It is the classic, quintessential Chaplin shot.

Both pathos and comedy are heightened in the next moments. A man comes and stands behind Charlie, unseen by him. At the bar the barkeep says

to Georgia (if we watch his mouth closely), "There's Charlie." She turns and says, "Charlie," smiles, and comes toward Chaplin. He's mystified but happy—until she goes right past him to greet the man behind him. Chaplin had used this idea of mistaken greetings before, notably in a two-reeler called *The Cure*, but only to be funny. Here it is funny, but it also crystallizes another matter: the moment of his falling in love despite his forlorn condition.

Georgia is played by Georgia Hale, whom Chaplin had seen in Josef von Sternberg's first film, *The Salvation Hunters*. Her career did not go on long after *The Gold Rush*, which is odd because her performance here is perfect—

Sole food: The starving Chaplin boils his shoe and makes a feast of it—carving it like a roast of beef (1), twirling the laces like spaghetti on his fork (2), and sucking the nails as if they were little bones (3).

1.

2.

3.

she supplies exactly the right qualities of sauciness, sex, and tenderness. Hale clearly plays the part with a knowledge of what is now called the "subtext," the meaning below the surface. This dance-hall girl is a prostitute; what else could she possibly be? (One of her friends at the dance hall is a beefy, older woman, with the look of the traditional madam.) Nothing is done or said to explicate this; it is simply there for those who can see it, and it deepens the film. Children, as I can remember from my own experience, see the characters as "innocent." Adults, however, can see that the other man resembles a prostitute's bully. Moreover, when Georgia and the other girls are playing in the snow one day near Charlie's cabin, an outing that leads to her discovery of his devotion, the sequence recalls the feeling of De Maupassant's "Madame Tellier's Establishment"—the staff of a bordello frisking on holiday.

The point of this subtext is not merely to slip innuendo past the censor. It provides, for those able to see it, a further stratum of reality for the *comedy* and, since the Tramp never recognizes what Georgia is, further proof of his armor of innocence. Others have noted that Chaplin pointedly chose to make a picture about a gold rush in the middle of the madly moneymaking twenties. He also chose to have the world beloved Tramp fall in love with, and finally win, a prostitute, in an American comedy—seemingly as a tacit certification of the postwar era's changing sexual standards.

During their encounter at the outing, Charlie invites Georgia and the other girls to New Year's Eve dinner in his cabin. They accept, knowing they won't come. On that evening, Charlie sets the table elaborately and prepares a big meal, then sits down to wait—and wait and wait. At last he nods off at the table and dreams that they have come, that all is joyous. In one of the most celebrated moments in all Chaplin films, Charlie dreams he is entertaining the adoring girls by doing the Oceana Roll. Sitting at the table, he sticks two forks into two sabot-shaped rolls, then

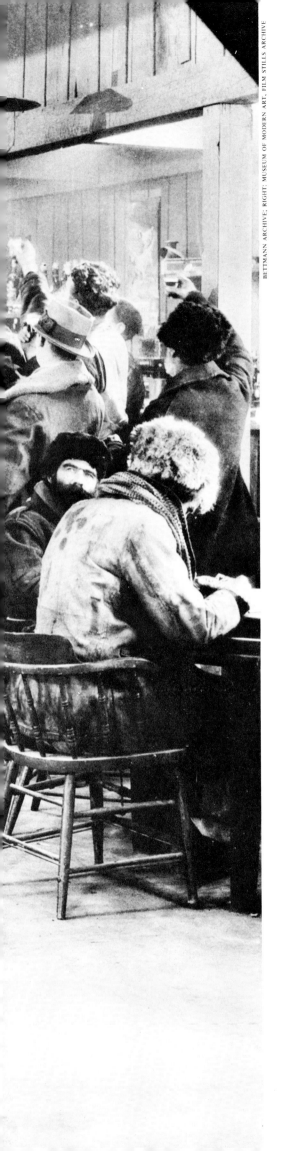

kicks and jigs them as if they were his legs and he were doing a chorus-girl dance. Every time I see this sequence coming, I think, "I know every move he's going to make. He can't possibly make me laugh again." And every time he does. One reason, deduced from the very last viewing, is that he doesn't merely kick his fork "legs," he uses his whole body behind the forks, employing utter concentration in miniature reproduction of a chorus girl's performance. And, typical of the picture's harmonics, this hilarious pantomime occurs in a dream into which the Tramp has fallen because he has been tricked and disappointed.

This dream dinner, we should also note, exemplifies another theme that runs through Chaplin's work, the mirror image of the hunger theme discussed earlier. Instead of hunger, we get the other extreme, the feast, the laden table, which has an effect in Chaplin films like the effect of feasts in Dickens (another man who knew poverty in London). Plentiful food does not mean gluttony, but love: an atmosphere of community, conviviality, and affection. One of the most touching moments in *The Kid* is the huge breakfast that the Kid prepares for himself and his "father," the Tramp. In *The Gold Rush*, the golden-brown turkey is the Tramp's contribution, even in a dream, to an atmosphere in which human beings can be human. Chaplin's idea of a low and dehumanized state is not hunger, but the insult to the full table. In *Modern Times*, the Tramp is strapped to an automatic feeding machine, with food enough but without feeling. It debases a daily joy.

I describe one more scene in *The Gold Rush* as an example of Chaplin's comic invention, though it is hard to limit one's self. When Charlie and Big Jim wake up in the lonely cabin to which they have returned, they don't realize, of course, that during the night the

In an uproarious Klondike saloon, the Lone Prospector watches Georgia Hale, the dance-hall girl atop the bar. In this famous shot, Chaplin puts the camera below eye level, silhouetting his own figure so that both he and Georgia stand apart—she on her pedestal, he alone on the periphery of the mob.

While their cabin, blown to the edge of a cliff, seesaws over the abyss, Charlie and Jim agonizingly inch up the tilting floor.

cabin was blown to a new location: the very edge of a cliff. They can't see out the frost-covered windows. As the cabin begins to shift on the precipice, Charlie decides to have a look at the trouble. He opens the back door—and, hanging onto the doorknob, swings out into immense space. If I had to vote for the single funniest sight gag in films, I'd probably choose this moment. Big Jim pulls Charlie back inside. Then comes a sequence in which the two men, one slight and the other burly, try to inch their way up the increasingly slanting floor toward the safe side of the cabin and the front door. It is a pearl of invisible dynamics, in which they cautiously *wish* their bodies upward.

Like so much in Chaplin's films, and in farce generally, this cabin sequence is built on danger, scary but seen from safety. The sequence is the quantum of the banana-peel gag, greatly multiplied: we know what it would feel like if it were happening to us, but we also know that it isn't. Comedy, of all kinds, supplies perception and superiority. In high comedy, which usually deals with social criticism, we can recognize hypocrisy or vanity, acknowledge secretly that we share it, and laugh with relief that it is being pilloried in someone else. In farce, the materials are often physical, often the dangers of daily life that surround us all the time. The *farceur* makes injury and possible death simultaneously real and unreal. We know that the Tramp and Big Jim will not be killed in the cabin—it simply

45

could not happen in this kind of picture; yet we feel the danger with our viscera. We are frightened at the same time that we are delighted by the skill of the artists who have outwitted death. Farce characters never get killed. They contrive for us a superiority over mortality, even as they make us laugh at their struggles to escape it.

To this comic heritage of danger combined with the subconscious assurance of safety, Chaplin adds a unique touch: grace. All through his career, it is manifest: as in the dangerous skating sequences of *The Rink* and *Modern Times*. One of the most famous remarks about Chaplin was made by W. C. Fields, himself a fine comedian of another sort. Fields, with salty verbal décor, said Chaplin was "the best ballet dancer that ever lived." What Fields omitted is that the ballet is often performed in the face of death.

The finish of *The Gold Rush* strengthens and resolves the light-dark harmonics of the whole. Some have objected to the ending because it is contrived to be happy, because the Tramp doesn't walk down the road alone at the end. But, as a matter of fact, that is *not* a typical ending of his feature films: *The Kid, City Lights,* and *Modern Times* also end happily. And if *The Gold Rush* was to have a happy ending, Charlie had to end up rich. Even this is not much different from *The Kid,* which finishes when the Tramp joins the Kid in the rich woman's house.

The Gold Rush differs only in that we *see* Charlie rich. Essential though the wealth is thematically, this was not the image that Chaplin wanted to leave before our eyes, so he devised a way for the rich Charlie to put on his Tramp clothes once again. This persona, resumed, gives Georgia, the prostitute, a chance to prove the genuineness of her feelings, and it gives Chaplin a chance to score a last point. The Tramp had to be dragged away from Georgia by Big Jim, had to be dragged to wealth; now the wealth brings them together again on the ship. Money and happiness, Chaplin seems to say, are the private

The Prospector gets the cold shoulder from Georgia, opposite, until Fate and the scenario at last reunite them on shipboard, above.

whims of two powers: Fate and authors.

But an even subtler complexity runs through the film, through most of his major films. The element that persists, through the comedy and through the pathos that makes the comedy beloved, is a sense of mystery. Who *is* the Tramp? What is the secret of his unique effect on us?

Consider. Here is a prospector who appears on a mountain trail wearing a wing collar and tie. We never question this, we never even really notice it. All right, perhaps that's because the Tramp's costume is by now an internationally accepted set of symbols. After he gets a job in the boom town, the Tramp, who has been collarless for a while, again wears a collar and tie. Even though this is a rough Alaskan town, we still don't notice the impossibility. When the Tramp and Big Jim are first snowbound in the cabin, Jim's whiskers grow and Charlie's don't.

But then the Tramp's incongruities move from costume into action, and we begin to wonder. When Georgia invites him to dance, he is wearing silly clothes and has wrapped one foot in rags to replace the eaten shoe. But he dances with exquisite style. Who *is* he? When he invites the girls to dinner, he not only knows how to cook, he knows all about table settings, party favors, dainty gift

wrappings, and etiquette. Who *is* he? When he performs the Oceana Roll, he knows a chorus-girl routine. Who *is* he? When Georgia's bullyboy tries to force his way into her room, Charlie chivalrously bars the door, contemptuous of danger. Again—who *is* he?

I propose no supernatural answer, that he is a divine messenger in ragged clothes, a fool of God. I do suggest that part of the genius of Chaplin, part of his superiority to all other film comics except Buster Keaton, is his ability to make us believe in a comic character whose standards are better than our own, just as his body in motion is more beautiful than our bodies. I suggest that one of the reasons we have loved him all these decades—and young people seem to feel that *they* have loved him for decades, too—is that he has not concentrated on merely making us laugh, but has shown us the funniness in a hero-clown, an unsententious agent of exemplary values. He is not dully angelic; he sometimes pulls off con games, though usually to a good end or to flout oppressive authority. But in the main he compensates for the shortcomings, social and physical, of our lives and beings. In his movement and in his code, even in his cunning, he is what we feel we ought to be.

In 1926 Bertolt Brecht wrote that he went to see *The Gold Rush,* after some delay, because it had made his theatre friends despondent about the theatre. He says that the picture made him share their despondency, but not because he felt there was a hierarchical difference between the arts of theatre and film. The difference was Chaplin. He says that Chaplin is an artist who "already qualifies as a historical event." Yes. *The Gold Rush* is a marvel, but it is Chaplin himself who is the landmark.

The Gold Rush is widely available in 16 mm. form. Among the firms from which it can be rented are: Brandon Films, 34 Mac-Questen Park Way South, Mount Vernon, New York 10550; Em Gee Film Library, 4931 Gloria Avenue, Encino, California 91316; and Janus Films, 745 Fifth Avenue, New York, New York 10022.

CONCERNING CLOWNS

Why do we need clowns? Perhaps because,
in Francis Bacon's words,
"There is in human nature generally more
of the fool than of the wise."

Of all the images that men have created for themselves, none is as equivocal, or as timeless, as the clown. He appears, of course, in many guises—as an acrobatic monkey, like Harlequin; as a half-witted servant, like Bertoldo of the Italian *commedia dell' arte;* as a melancholy tramp, like Emmett Kelly's Weary Willie. But even more remarkable, and perplexing, than all these contradictory guises is the fact that a clown no sooner fits a convention than he violates it. The moment we have described him as the butt of the joke, he turns around to do the butting. Too hopelessly awkward to climb a stepladder because his left foot is pressing on his right one, the clown begins to topple over—and then double-somersaults to the ground in a prodigy of graceful acrobatics. As soon as we have seen him for the coarse practical joker he is, he turns out to be a sighing romantic. Like man himself, the clown is a mass of grotesque inconsistencies.

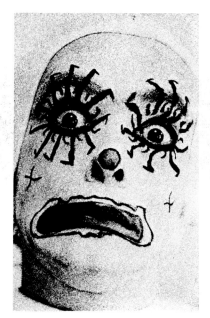

The clowns shown on these pages in the expressive photographs of Herbert Migdoll are clowns of a very special kind—engaged in what appears to be a most unclownlike exercise in frenzy and terror. They are, first of all, clowns of the elegant Pierrot variety, with flour-whitened faces and white suits and ruffs. They are, secondly, not real clowns but ballet dancers playing clowns, and belong, not to the circus, but to the City Center Joffrey Ballet in New York. The ballet they are performing is *The Clowns,* a macabre parable of nuclear holocaust and universal destruction created by Gerald Arpino, one of America's finest young choreographers.

What, it may be asked, do clowns have to do with nuclear war, with a ballet that opens with dead bodies glowing radioactively onstage as bombs burst, a ballet that closes with a grim dance of death as the reborn clowns envelope themselves in a great plastic balloon and destroy themselves once more? Why should a clown, bringer of mirth, be employed as a bringer of ruin, and why should his endearing love of foolish things like balloons be made a metaphor of terror?

Arpino's clowns evince what is perhaps the oddest contradiction of the clown: while he is usually a figure of fun, there is always something threatening about his fooling. Take the circus clown who rushes, all eagerness, to help the roustabouts put up the paraphernalia for the next act. The workers tug on a rope, he tangles them in it; they lift a heavy weight, he lets it fall cruelly on their heads. Every object a clown touches takes on a malignant life of its own—the plastic balloons become weapons in Arpino's ballet—as if the clowns were a source of evil or a conduit for demonic forces. To children, whom clowns frighten as well as amuse, it would come as no surprise that Harlequin, the leading

TEXT CONTINUED ON PAGE 57

A PORTFOLIO OF PHOTOGRAPHS BY HERBERT MIGDOLL

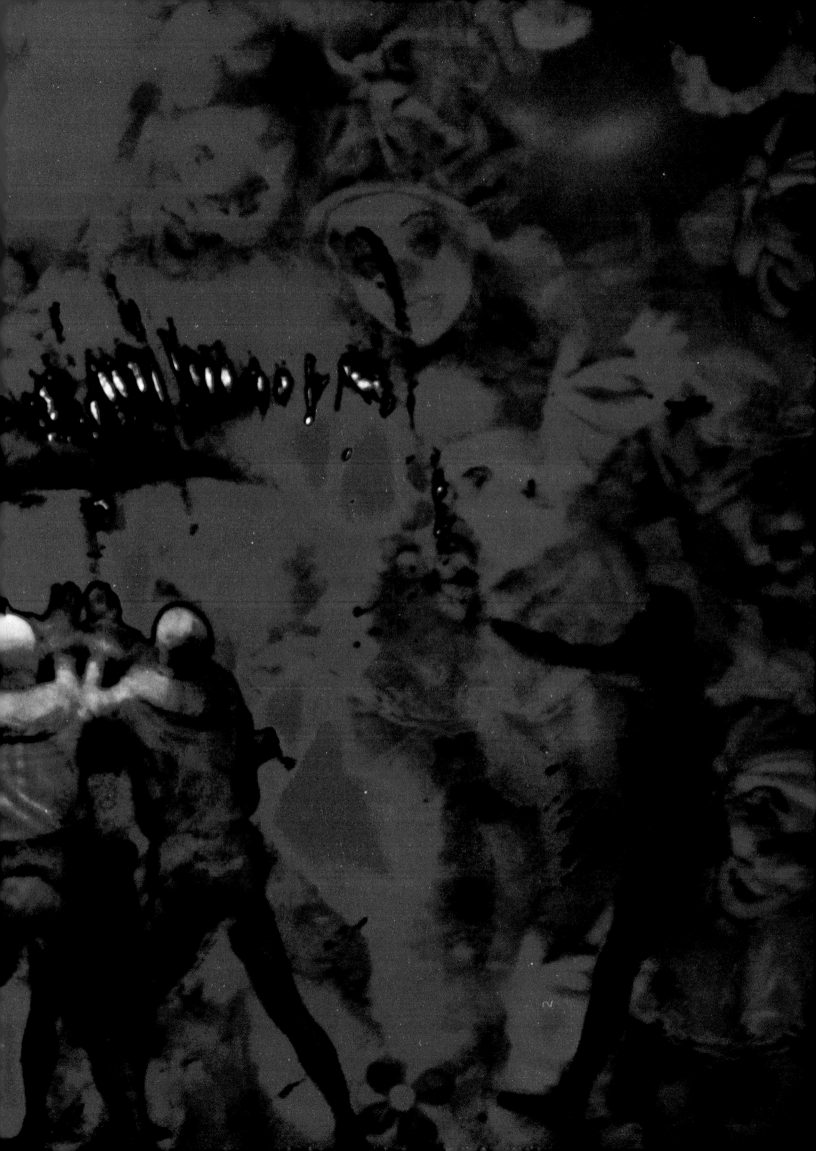

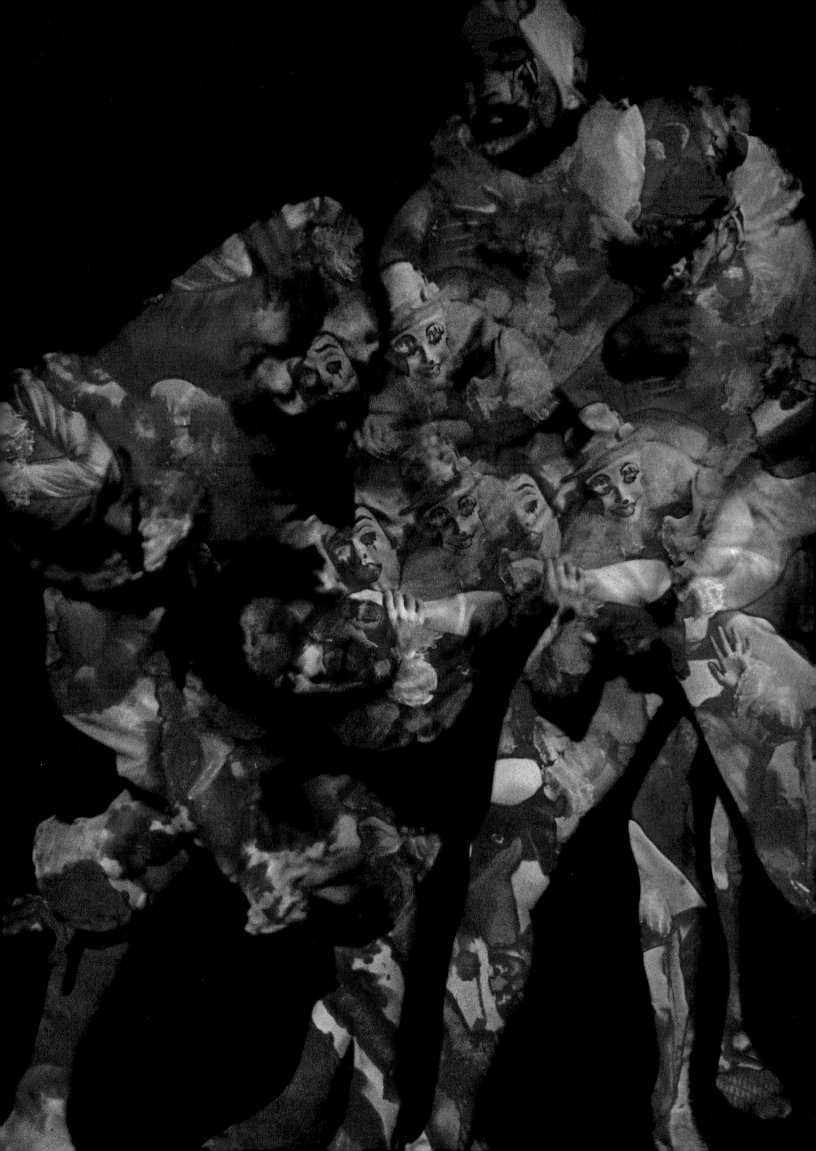

TEXT CONTINUED FROM PAGE 48

character of the *commedia dell' arte,* began life in the Middle Ages as a figure of the Devil. The wickedness of Arpino's ballet clowns, who, in their frenzied folly, try to kill the clown who has given them life, is no merciless modern conceit. The sinister is an inherent element in clowning: even the most innocent of circus clowns makes his grease-paint mouth a diabolic leer.

No clown can be exclusively one thing or another, butt or knave, oaf or acrobat, ninny or fox, innocent or evil, for then he would cease being a clown and become merely a character. Thus Arpino's sinister clowns are beautifully dressed. And thus, Chaplin, the greatest clown of the twentieth century, got kicked but kicked back, moved with wondrous grace yet shuffled in outsized shoes, stole hot dogs from street vendors and shy glances at fair maidens, and sported a dandy's walking stick as well as baggy trousers. The clown embodies the central truth that there is no such predictable being as "Man" but only a plurality of men, that every definition of Man is false. It is because the possible combinations of oaf and dancer, dolt and fox, dupe and dupester, glutton and swain, are infinite that no two clowns—like no two men—are ever exactly alike, although each and every one plays the fool.

A clown, in the end, has only one fixed attribute, his indestructibility. He never learns, he never changes, he is irredeemably what he is, a fool. He wreaks havoc and brings down the roof, but he survives. At the

Gerald Arpino rehearses members of the Joffrey Ballet for The Clowns, *above. Plastic inflatables, created for the ballet and choreographed along with the dancers, lie on the stage.*

beginning of Arpino's ballet only one clown has survived the nuclear devastation, and at the end, when the other clowns have danced themselves into their inflated plastic coffin, he again survives. How is it that this one fool is able to escape the common folly? Because—and this, too, is the lesson of the clown—there is no such thing as the common folly; there are only individual fools. And so Arpino's ballet, for all its terrors and threats of nuclear holocaust, has a bizarrely happy message.   w.k.

The Herbert Migdoll photograph opposite and those on the preceding pages are images of the ballet that no ballet audience has ever seen. How to capture the spectacle of the human figure dancing is a problem that has fascinated artists at least as far back as Edgar Dégas, who spent some of his most brilliant hours sketching at the ballet. As today's foremost dance photographer, Mr. Migdoll's aims may be similar to the painter's, but his tools are more complicated. He uses several techniques to achieve his effects, among them solarization, a controlled exposure of film to light to produce vivid colors; and montage, the combination of two or more images. His pictures of another Joffrey Ballet production, *Astarte,* appeared in the Spring, 1971, issue of HORIZON. These photographs of *The Clowns*—briefly described in sequence below—reveal the frivolity, the terror, and the beauty of Arpino's ballet.

1) Painted clowns have come to life after a nuclear holocaust. 2) They cavort gaily, but their faces merge with that of an anguished clown. 3) Tiring of their play, they begin to get rough with the clown who has given them life, danced by Gary Chryst (center). 4) They toss their creator toward a huge plastic balloon, which later envelops them in death. 5) The "bodies" that lay on the stage at the beginning of the ballet suddenly, as if electrified, start to dance. 6) The attempted murder of the central clown and earlier playful antics combine in an eerie montage. 7) Nightmarish images appear to spring from the head of a lonely and sad-faced Pierrot.

THE TERRORISTS

"Madness alone is truly terrifying." —Joseph Conrad

Terrorism appears to be a specific malady of modern civilization. No other society, we tend to assume, has suffered to the same extent from precisely the same social and moral pestilence. This assumption is wrong, if we apply the dictionary definition of terrorism literally, yet not entirely wrong. For terrorism as we know it today is, in fact, a relatively new phenomenon in world history. Its embryonic forms date back less than a hundred years.

To be sure, methods of terror, more or less systematically employed, either as instruments of tyranny or as weapons against it, are as old as organized society. Nero and Ivan the Terrible were both undeniably terrorists in the literal sense. So, on the insurrectionary side, was Guy Fawkes, who hoped to destroy what he thought of as a repressive anti-Catholic regime in England by setting off barrels of gunpowder in the cellar of Parliament while King James I was present at a session. So, too, were the guerrilla outlaws of the Balkan Peninsula, who through the dark centuries of Ottoman oppression helped keep alive the spirit of freedom among the subject peoples of southeastern Europe.

So, in every age, were many others: rulers and rebels, heroes, inquisitors, and assassins; sometimes acting as mass killers or torturers, but always sowers of terror, and all therefore terrorists.

But none of them were quite the same as the skyjackers, the letter bombers, the kidnappers and murderers, the street snipers, the parkers of booby-trapped automobiles near school playgrounds, the saboteurs of waterworks or power lines on which the life of a city may depend, and the knockers on doors in the night, in or out of uniform, that the word "terrorist" conjures up in our minds today. The difference is subtle but unmistakable, not so much in the scale or degree of the terror as in its moral texture.

A comparison of two famous acts of terrorism underscores the difference, and at the same time illuminates its nature. The first case is that of Vera Zasulich, an idealistic young Russian socialist who, in January, 1878, shot and seriously wounded General Fedor Trepov, the St. Petersburg prefect of police. The mechanism of the crime was simple. Though she had already been sentenced to exile for earlier contacts with

the student underground, and would later became a prominent figure in revolutionary circles, Vera Zasulich planned and executed the deed without accomplices. Evidently a no-nonsense sort of young woman, she solicited an interview with the prefect, drew a revolver as she walked into his office, and opened fire.

Her motive, as explained in court, was equally straightforward, and as rationally thought out as the motive for any murderous violence can be. Trepov was known to be particularly brutal and ruthless. Recently he had outraged the moral susceptibilities of Russian liberals and revolutionaries—and, indeed, of most civilized Russians—by having a prisoner flogged a hundred lashes for failing to stand up in his presence during a tour of inspection. Moreover, the victim, a student, had been a political prisoner, and though the knout was frequently used on common criminals, "politicals" had so far been spared this barbarity. Vera Zasulich had felt that such a grave offense to human dignity cried out for punishment; since no legal redress was possible under the czarist despotism, she

By EDMOND TAYLOR

took the law into her own hands. The jury, sharing her indignation, promptly acquitted her, and her revolutionary admirers later managed to get her out of the country before the police could seize her on some new pretext. (The remarkable and unforeseen display of civic courage on the part of the St. Petersburg jurors, incidentally, so infuriated the czarist authorities that Alexander II was led to sign a fateful decree abolishing jury trails for terrorists and subversives throughout Russia.)

The moral climate of this incident is so exotic from the twentieth-century point of view that a contemporary reader may feel inclined to ask, where is the terrorism? Although Vera Zasulich no doubt hoped her assault on Trepov would give other Russian officials food for reflection, it would be exaggeration to accuse her of trying to terrorize them, or anyone. The terrorist, if any, was the uniformed bully she shot at.

In nineteenth-century usage, however, attacks on the official establishment were conventionally termed acts of terror, and their perpetrators were *ipso facto* terrorists. Underlying the verbal convention lay a common pool of genuine fear: the obsessive nineteenth-century bourgeois dread of anything that threatened to disturb the social order. If nothing else, an "act of terror," even one committed in another country, might unsettle the bourse—a prospect that toward the close of the century filled the numerous holders of Russian state debentures with an almost religious horror. It was thus because she frightened the investors in Russia's backwardness—whether their investment was financial, diplomatic, or simply emotional—that Vera Zasulich deserves to be called a terrorist.

Terror and intimidation were, then, the side effect, rather than the primary aim, of numerous later acts of terrorism. There are no such semantic complications, however, in the act of twentieth-century terrorism contrasted with the Zasulich case: the massacre at Israel's Lod Airport on May 30, 1972. Three terrorists in the service of the

Popular Front for the Liberation of Palestine (or a subgroup affiliated with it), debarking from an international flight, managed to smuggle submachine guns into the passenger terminal and empty their chargers at random in the crowded lobby, killing twenty-six persons and wounding seventy-six others. Sixteen of the dead were Puerto Rican pilgrims visiting the Holy Land.

From the organizer's point of view the Lod massacre was rational, or at least in accord with the logic of terrorism. It was intended to shock the world, thus focusing international attention on the Palestinian problem, and it did. It was aimed to hurt Israel—psychologically by shaking Israeli pride and self-confidence, economically by damaging the Israeli tourist industry—and it probably did. Perhaps it was meant, like a number of terrorist outrages in all ages, to provoke the adversary into some self-damaging over-reaction. If so, it was at least partly successful: the Israeli reprisal attacks on Lebanon, where the Palestinian guerrillas were based, in all likelihood did the Israeli cause more harm than good. Finally, the attack was revenge for the failure of a Palestinian attempt to hijack a Belgian airliner, three weeks earlier, en route to the same Israeli airport—a dramatic affair in which the

Israeli Army paratroopers had killed two Arab hijackers and captured two others. All this sounds paranoid, to say the least, but lucid enough in the context of present-day terrorism.

The psychology of the three gunmen is another matter. Here we enter a stoned world, that is, one of stoned thoughts and feelings. All three terrorists were Japanese. Naturally the first question that arises is why three young Japanese revolutionaries, whatever their ideology or sympathies, undertook a mission that was manifestly a kamikaze one, as well as blindly murderous, on behalf of a group of Palestinian irredentists. The answer, in a stoned world, of course, is why not? But the Israeli military investigators and judges who questioned the sole survivor of the trio, Kozo Okamoto, a twenty-four-year-old former university student, were incapable of eliciting such an elementary response from him. At his trial Okamoto appeared to be a tired and not very articulate young man, drained of all emotion except a residual bitterness at the cruel trick he thought the Israelis had played on him: his first examiner had promised he could die when he told everything he knew, and now they were saying he had to live. (He was finally sentenced to life imprisonment.) "My mouth is unable to tell you what I feel,"

THE BEGINNING: *In January, 1878, Vera Zasulich shoots General Fedor Trepov in St. Petersburg.*

he told the judge who kept questioning him about his motives. Asked what he hoped to achieve by his participation in the massacre, he replied, no doubt truthfully, "Nothing." He had killed, he stated, because he had been ordered to kill. "As a member of the great international army of revolution," he amplified a little, "I was prepared to do anything for the cause."

This cause was defined by him simply as "world revolution on behalf of the world proletariat" (not revolution of the proletariat itself as in the Marxist formulation). One might as well call it the revolution without a name, the anything revolution. And the international revolutionary army to which Okamoto said he belonged is no part of the Third, Fourth, or any other organized International. Devoid of an authentically internationalist doctrine, it is merely a kind of revolutionary kinship group, based on affinities of style or temper rather than on ideological concordance, which incorporates underground activists in several countries.

Okamoto had been recruited for—or assigned to—the struggle against Israeli "imperialism," a revolutionary cause supported by some of the most reactionary elements in the Arab world, under an exchange and co-operation agreement negotiated a few months earlier between Japanese left-wing extremists and an agent of the Palestinian underground. He had demonstrated that he was ready to sacrifice himself in this ideologically ambiguous combat, but he probably would have been equally ready to die for a united Catholic Ireland, an independent Quebec, or possibly even for a Peronist Argentina. Fanatical commitment to a revolutionary cause so vague that it is interchangeable with almost any other is one of the characteristic traits of the modern terrorist.

Even more distinctive of the new terrorism is the random nature of its violence. Earlier terrorists usually had some specific and comprehensible grievance against their victims. Quite often the attack was in retaliation for acts of exceptional violence or cruelty, e.g., Vera Zasulich's attempt to shoot Gen. Trepov. Even the crowned heads, cabinet ministers, or high administrative officials who were assassinated, so to speak *ex officio*, had generally singled themselves out as particularly hateful representatives of a hated class or nation. Innocent bystanders were sometimes sacrificed, but most often the terrorists took special pains to avoid endangering them, even at considerable risk to their own lives. Before the young Russian Socialist Revolutionary Ivan Kaliaiev succeeded in assassinating the czar's uncle, Grand Duke Sergius, the heavy-handed military governor of Moscow, in 1905, he twice in the same night waited in the street with a camouflaged bomb in his hands, and twice held back from throwing it, because the grand duchess and some of her nephews and nieces were also riding in the grand duke's carriage.

In the Lod massacre, however, innocent bystanders were the primary target, for in all probability the airport crowd would consist of Israeli civilians with no direct responsibility for their government's policies and even foreign tourists completely uninvolved in the Arab-Israeli vendetta. The comment attributed (by a responsible French weekly) to Dr. George Habache, head of the Palestinian PFL and presumptive organizer of the operation—"There are no innocent tourists"—might indicate an almost clinically irrational hatred. Such hatreds do unquestionably underlie many acts of terrorism today, but the minds behind those of the Palestinian terrorists, however twisted they may be, have repeatedly demonstrated a keen sense of psychological strategy. There is good reason to believe that both the Lod raid and the still more spectacular kidnapping of nine members of the Israel Olympic team at Munich by commandos of the Black September organization some three months later were deliberately planned to produce the impression of irrational, almost maniacal violence. Consciously, or unconsciously, the planners of the two outrages put into effect the strategy of the absurd that Mr. Vladimir, the cynical, civilized embassy secretary in Conrad's *The Secret Agent,* lays down for his anarchist *agent provocateur,* Mr. Verloc. Vladimir orders him to perpetrate "an act of destructive ferocity so absurd as to be incomprehensible, inexplicable, almost unthinkable: in fact, mad." Such madness seems the most terrifying form of violence, Conrad's diplomat goes on to explain, because "you cannot placate it either by threats, persuasion, or bribes." He might also have added that madness, like lightning, is unpredictable; no one can foresee where it will strike next. The letter bombs, addressed to Jewish business or professional men of many nationalities, a number of them seemingly picked at random from the pages of a directory, represent probably the widest application of the principle of unpredictability in the annals of terrorism.

The Palestinians appear to have made the strategy of the absurd their speciality: the sheer audacity of their most spectacular exploits seems to flout our criteria of rational behavior. Other present-day terrorists in Europe, Latin America, or Canada, however, often practice the same basic strategy. Human victims are not absolutely indispensable—Conrad's Mr. Verloc was instructed only to blow up the Greenwich Observatory, the sanctuary of the modern goddess Time—but shedding blood, especially innocent blood, adds to the impression of insane violence that the primary outrage is intended to convey. If mass slaughter is impractical, the desired effect can still be achieved by sacrificing a modest number of victims, or even a single victim, in some particularly bizarre and horrible way. At least a provisional record in the field of beastliness was set by the mysterious Spanish terrorists who, in November, 1972, invaded the French consulate in Saragossa, tied the consul to his chair, daubed him with red paint, poured gasoline on his clothes, and left an incendiary bomb in his office that went off before he could free himself. This piece of gratuitous sadism, according to the Spanish police, was intended as a protest against some relatively mild restrictions the French government had recently placed on Spanish political refugees in France.

To understand the whole nightmare of modern terrorism, we must look at the ideological factors and acts of past terrorism, asking certain basic questions. How did present-day terrorism develop? When did the features that distinguish it from earlier forms of terror first appear? What, in particular, are the origins of the seemingly lunatic but rigorously logical strategy of the absurd that appears to inspire its most atrocious manifestations?

Completely satisfactory answers to these questions would entail a total autopsy of modern civilization. In large measure, contemporary terrorism is a direct reflection of the ideological fanaticisms, the kinky intellectual trends, the decay of public and private moral standards, the flight from reason, and the general dehumanization that afflict our age. What has happened to terrorism in our century is akin to what has happened to crime or to war. When politicians routinely order that antipersonnel bombs be dropped on crowded civilian centers in an undeclared war, why be surprised when terrorists gun down women and children as a form of revolutionary propaganda? When intellectuals make a cult of the stoned mind, why shouldn't terrorism attract the cultists of stoned violence?

Of course, certain trends of modern society and certain currents of modern thought have contributed more directly than others to shaping the patterns of twentieth-century terrorism. Frantz Fanon's concept of therapeutic violence—aggravated by Sartre's embroideries on the theme, as Hannah Arendt has pointed out—has had a significant

BLACK TERROR: *Bombs explode; the Bonnot gang threatens France.*

influence, especially in ex-colonial regions. Trotsky's apology for revolutionary terror, including such barbarous practices as shooting hostages, has been carried by some New Left thinkers to extremes that would probably have horrified Trotsky himself. Above all, distorted interpretations of Marx's class-war doctrine have been blended with run-to-seed social Darwinism to depict the revolutionary's bourgeois enemy as a subhuman type whose extermination by any means is justifiable. As early as 1907 a Russian Maximalist intellectual named Pavlov (not *the* Pavlov) published a booklet entitled *Purification of the Human Race,* which described a "race" of exploiters with innate "negative traits" resembling those of the gorilla and the orangutan. All the representatives of this pernicious breed, Pavlov declared, should be "exterminated like cockroaches."

Important as the ideology undoubtedly is, however, some of the key episodes in the history of modern terrorism are no less essential to a true understanding of its present social implications. To begin with, the word itself has an instructive history. It comes not from "terror" but from The Terror, that of the French Revolution. Used by Robespierre's enemies after they had guillotined him, it was a pejorative for the fallen dictator's policies and apologists. Soon it became the pretext for launching a new reign of terror against the "terrorists" themselves. Thus the first terrorists were not subversives trying to overthrow a regime, but men in power using police violence to defend the state.

Every act of terrorism begins, in the eyes of its practitioners, as an instance of counterterrorism. The most murderous cases of terrorism in this century have ostensibly been counterterroristic measures by the police in Stalin's Russia and Hitler's Germany; and the special kind of love-hate relationship that exists between the policeman and the revolutionary terrorist, each in a sense indispensable to the other, has been a vital influence in conditioning the professional psychology of both.

The police factor was particularly significant in the evolution of the terrorist syndrome that developed in Russia in the second half of the nineteenth century. Revolutionary terrorism made its earliest appearance there during the wave of repression and political reaction that swept the country after the unsuccessful nationalist insurrection of 1863 in Russian Poland. The reign of Alexander II had begun in a euphoric atmosphere of progress and social reform, but the Polish uprising, along with intensified pressure from the reactionary elements in Russian society, pushed Alexander and the czarist ad-

NORTHERN IRELAND: *Men, women, and children slaughter their neighbors in a bloody civil war.*

ministration sharply to the right. The socialist and populist idealists who up to then had conceived the transformation of Russian despotism as a gradual process to be brought about by educating the masses found themselves subject to increasing police harassment. From reformers they rapidly turned into revolutionaries; the more energetic ones organized underground groups and resorted to terrorism.

Though there was an attempt to kill the czar as early as 1866, the first generation of Russian terrorists generally confined their activities to executing traitors or police spies in their own ranks and to reprisals for the tortures, floggings, and hangings of an increasingly harsh repression. In 1879, however, a split in the revolutionary underground led to the formation of an extremist group called *Narodnaia Volia,* the Will of the People. Its program called for "terrorist activity to remove the most important personalities belonging to the Administration . . . This will have as a general aim the weakening and demoralization of the Administration. . . . the strengthening of popular belief in the party's ultimate success, and finally the inculcation of a fighting spirit." The Will of the People thus became the first terrorist organization in the modern sense.

Dominated by two implacable personalities, Andrei Zhelyabov, the son of a serf, a bearded giant with hypnotic eyes, and Sophia Perovskaia, the daughter of a former high czarist of-

ficial, a young girl with a pink-and-cream complexion, a childish face, and the reproving look of a governess, the Will of the People decided to strike the autocracy at its head. After two unsuccessful attempts to assassinate Alexander II by blowing up his private train, the conspirators succeeded on February 5, 1880, in setting off a heavy charge of dynamite in the cellar of the Winter Palace, directly under the czar's dining room, at exactly the hour he normally took his evening meal. Due to an unforeseen delay in his daily schedule, Alexander once more escaped death, but eleven members of the palace staff were killed and fifty-six wounded. The news of this unprecedented act created a sensation throughout Europe.

A year later the terrorists finally killed Alexander with a bomb thrown at his carriage. Instead of shaking the Russian autocracy to its foundations, the assassination intensified reaction and repression—which, in turn, aggravated revolutionary violence. The Will of the People was decimated by the arrest of its leading members. Five of them, including Zhelyabov and Sophia Perovskaia, were hanged. Their trial and execution etched in the Russian mind the romantic image of the revolutionary secret avenger—hero-martyr and self-sacrificing assassin—that a long line of modern intellectuals, from Turgenev to Camus, has universalized and romanticized. Today, more than ever, the image fascinates violent and idealistic young imaginations. The an-

archists of the 1880's and 1890's, especially the French ones, were among the chief forgers both of the modern terrorist ethos and of basic terrorist strategy. The cult of revolutionary destruction preached by Mikhail Bakunin, the nineteenth-century ideologue who is probably closest in spirit to the far-left terrorists of the present, undoubtedly influenced the generation that followed him. So—though the debt was rarely acknowledged—did Bakunin's masterful disciple, Serge Nechaiev, who said that the only valid criterion of revolutionary morality is the effectiveness of revolutionary action. But both Nechaiev (whose philosophy of revolution had more appeal to the early Bolsheviks than to the anarchists) and Bakunin, not himself a terrorist in the present sense, were soon left far behind by the anarchist school of "propaganda by the deed" that sprang up after the latter's death in 1876.

In the more extreme anarchist circles there gradually developed a sect of what might almost literally be called dynamite worshipers. A song once popular in the ill-lighted, absinthe-reeking Montmartre cabarets patronized by Bohemian intellectuals and authentic working class anarchists expresses this mystique of salvational violence:

> Comrades, I am Father Purge,
> Pharmacist to humanity,
> My pills are sure to give the urge—
> Prescribed by Doctor Equality.

> My shelves are stocked with fulminate;
> Saltpetre too you'll surely find,
> Gunpowder, nitro, and picrate
> Enough to clean the poisoned mind.

Though the French anarchists, unlike the early Russian populists, were free to spread their ideas openly, they, too, often reacted to police violence. The first bomb outrage to rock the French capital was planned as a direct reprisal for the brutal repression of a May Day demonstration in 1891. It wrecked the private apartment of the presiding judge, who had imposed a heavy prison sentence on one of the demonstrators. Shortly afterward the flat occupied by the public prosecutor in the same trial was blown up. The author of the bombings, an ex-bandit named François Ravachol, who had been converted by reading anarchist literature to what he considered a form of disinterested public service, was finally arrested and sentenced to prison; he was then tried again for the first of three purely mercenary murders committed before his conversion to the anarchist cause, and finally guillotined. Now the anarchists had a new martyr, and another wave of bombings struck the capital, leading frightened bourgeois to clamor for measures of still greater severity to be taken in repressing terrorism.

While counting on the strategy of the Big Bang to disorganize bourgeois society, anarchist publications of the period also offered their readers practical hints for furthering the cause at the village or household level. "Burn down or blow up churches," advised *La Lutte Sociale* ("The Social Struggle"). "Poison fruit and vegetables and offer them to the priests. Do the same with the big landowners. Let servants season the dishes of the bourgeoisie with poison. Let the peasant kill the rural constable with his shotgun." According to Emile Marenssin, a specialist on revolutionary violence, in the year 1892 alone some five hundred acts of terrorism occurred in the Western Hemisphere and more than a thousand in Europe.

The most spectacular exploits of anarchist terrorism in nineteenth-century France were probably the assassination of President Sadi Carnot in 1894, the bomb thrown from a public gallery onto the floor of the Chamber of Deputies in 1892 (causing a number of flesh wounds, but no deaths or permanent injuries), and the explosion in a crowded Paris café in 1894 that killed one customer and wounded some twenty others. This last outrage was perhaps the most significant psychologically. Its author, Emile Henry, a well-educated young man from a respectable bourgeois family, who for unknown reasons had turned into an anarchist fanatic, walked into the Café Terminus, a large es-

tablishment near the St. Lazare station, pulled a small but powerful homemade bomb out of his overcoat pocket, and threw it directly at the orchestra, which was playing on a dais in the middle of the room.

At his trial Henry explained with some pride how he had constructed his bomb according to approved scientific principles and had methodically rehearsed his crime. He was less articulate about why he had picked that particular target. The Terminus was not Maxim's, a symbol of the brazenly flaunted luxury of the people's exploiters. It specialized in offering "good" music—the orchestra was playing Vincent d'Indy when Henry's bomb went off—to modestly paid white-collar workers seeking culture. From the contempt in Henry's voice it was evident that he despised his victims' musical taste and cultural pretensions, but if he was indulging the whim of a secret tyrant by his act, it was the whim of a Torque-

mada rather than that of a Nero.

Exemplary punishment seems to have been Henry's aim—punishment for the crime of collaborating with a hateful system by submitting to exploitation and for trying to console oneself with the small pleasures that the exploiters allowed their slaves. His only regret, he said, was that there were not more dead. "But those were innocent victims that you struck!" one of the three judges exclaimed. Henry's reply explicitly formulated for the first time in modern terrorist annals the typically paranoid dogma of collective guilt that is now regularly invoked in order to justify indiscriminate or absurdist acts of terrorism: "There are no innocent victims."

The arrogant, callous, almost senseless crime in the Café Terminus, followed some years later by the emergence of the Bonnot gang—motorized bandits who professed anarchist convictions but likewise robbed and

THE LOD MASSACRE: *Twenty-six die in a senseless act of terror—"There are no innocent tourists."*

murdered for their personal enrichment —discredited terrorism as a revolutionary weapon in the eyes of the French working class. Even the usual police overreaction failed to produce new sympathizers for the anarchist cause. The progressive moral deterioration of the so-called Black Terror in France illustrates the general pattern for clandestine organizations that rely primarily on acts of criminal violence to achieve their objectives: idealists launch what they view as a struggle for justice; violence escalates in reaction to opposing violence; in the end the gangsters and the psychopaths take over.

Not all terrorist movements degenerate so radically. When freedom of speech and assembly are respected, and police overreaction is kept within bounds by the law, the degeneration may take a positive form: a progression from real violence to purely rhetorical violence. Military discipline, even that maintained in a guerrilla force, checks pathological degeneration in some, but not all, cases. If the terrorists feel they have the moral support of the community within which they operate, they may resist the psychological forces that tend to desocialize and dehumanize them. However, terrorist groups that

have no significant community support, or that feel their support is slipping, are particularly tempted to employ inhuman extremes of violence.

Degeneration, moreover, does not always take the same forms. The Combat Organization set up within the Socialist Revolutionary party in Russia at the beginning of this century carried out terrorist operations on an unprecedented scale. Its victims included, besides the Grand Duke Sergius, two ministers of the interior and an impressive list of high police officials and provincial governors. A large number of its members succeeded, however, in maintaining a relatively high standard of professional morality—for that particular profession. But little by little, terrorism, instead of being considered a mere adjunct to other forms of revolutionary activity, came to be thought of as an end in itself. The resulting obsession with security and conspiratorial technique facilitated the rise to leadership within the Combat Organization of a crack professional named Evno Azev, who encouraged the tendency to make violence for the sake of violence the group's only goal.

Azev was a thick-chested, bushy-bearded engineer and undoubtedly an

artist, even a genius, in his own line. He had been planted in the party as an *agent provocateur* by the Okhrana, the political and security section of the czarist police, with the specific mission of penetrating its terrorist wing. He succeeded so well that he eventually became its top planner. Azev failed to mention this promotion to his police employers, though he did betray into their hands a number of his comrades, and for years the Okhrana never realized that its own prize agent had planned and instigated the assassination of the czar's uncle and of its departmental chief, V. K. Plehve. Azev often sabotaged terrorist operations of secondary importance by giving the Okhrana accurate advance warning, but on the big spectaculars his information was too vague or too late to save the victim. Even when the organization hatched plots to assassinate Nicholas II, Azev, though he reported the news, held back vital details that were needed to assure the czar's protection. It was only through a series of accidents that the plot aborted. Finally unmasked as a double agent, first by the revolutionaries, and later by the Okhrana, Azev evaded the vengeance of both.

The anecdote is more than a picturesque footnote to the general history of modern terrorism. It illustrates the almost universal vulnerability of terrorist organizations to infiltration by the police or the secret service, and the lengths to which the latter will sometimes go to preserve the cover of a double agent. When the *agent provocateur* in a terrorist group is employed by an internal security service, he is generally told to avoid actually provoking violence, or even participating directly in any criminal act; but such instructions are nearly always platonic. And in some instances, literal provocation is, in fact, the police aim. Though documentary proof is incomplete, several French historians are convinced that the Paris police, operating through an undercover agent, supplied the anarchist Auguste Vaillant with the bomb that he threw in the Chamber of Deputies.

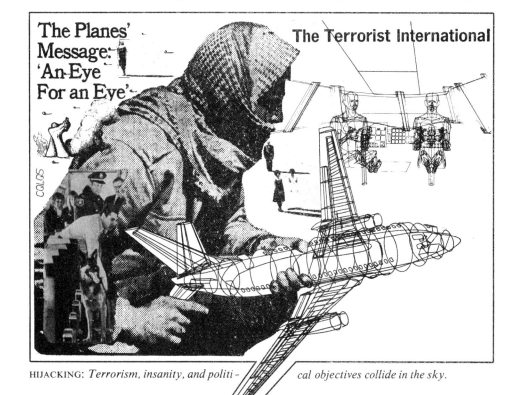

The Planes' Message: 'An Eye For an Eye'

The Terrorist International

COLOS

HIJACKING: *Terrorism, insanity, and political objectives collide in the sky.*

When a terrorist organization is manipulated through double agents working for a foreign, rather than a domestic, secret service, the acts of terror thus provoked are likely to be both spectacular and explosive. Such manipulation, no doubt aimed at sabotaging any negotiations between Israel and her Arab neighbors, may account for the Khartoum outrage in which the U.S. ambassador and the Belgian chargé d'affaires were murdered. And the wildest, most extreme acts of terrorism may develop when a double agent with a mind of his own, like Azev, tries to play one of his masters against the other.

Azev is important for another reason, underlined by the Soviet historian Roy Medvedev in his monumental study of Stalinist tyranny. The double agent of the Azev type is the psychological as well as symbolic link between the revolutionary and the police or totalitarian forms of terrorism. Medvedev rejects the charge that Stalin was himself a double agent employed by the Okhrana at the time he was holding up banks and participating in other terrorist acts ordered by Lenin's secret Bolshevik troika. But citing the studies of two Soviet colleagues, Medvedev brings out the similarities of character between Azev and Stalin, each distinguished by an immeasurable and uninhibited lust for power. Though Stalin's real name probably never figured on any police roster of double agents, he played a double-agent's role, concealing his real goals from his comrades, while he was ruthlessly manipulating them to further his own ends.

Azev, according to Medvedev, particularly enjoyed proving to himself his ability to outwit everyone else. He savored the secret power of life or death he held over his comrades by being able to periodically betray a certain number of them to the hangman. Stalin, as dictator, derived a similar satisfaction from sending his old party comrades to the firing squad, starting with his former rivals and his intellectual superiors, and continuing until all of Russia was in a permanent state of terror.

SAVAGE REPRISAL: *Black Septembrists kidnap nine members of the Israeli Olympic team.*

The Azev-Stalin comparison shows the basic structural similarities between the revolutionary type of terrorism that gives us such horrors as the Lod massacre and the totalitarian mass terrorism that gave us Stalin's show trials and cellar executions. There is one important difference, however, that Medvedev glosses over: caution was one of Stalin's dominant traits, while Azev's career as a double agent was an endless game of Russian roulette.

Of the two it is the Azev type that is more relevant to the terrorist threat as it presents itself in the world today. Our complex technological civilization offers many targets for the saboteur, and the imaginative terrorist can use such modern tools as plastic explosives, the submachine gun, and the jumbo-jet airliner—not to mention the TV camera. Imagine a present-day Azev with all these tools at his disposal, plus some of the simpler weapons in the arsenal of biological warfare. And, finally, there is the danger that a terrorist group might some day manage to steal a nuclear bomb or warhead. What an opportunity for the fanatics, the death cultists, and the amateurs of Russian roulette on the planetary scale.

That is why we need, not a new Holy Alliance to stamp out terrorism, nor a pious, unenforceable UN resolution condemning its crimes, but practical, if limited, international co-operation to contain its menace. If we can stop terrorists from massacring or ransoming innocent travelers at will, and deny them access to the weapons of mass destruction that might some day enable them to perpetrate a world holocaust, that is as much as we can hope for. But whether we can or cannot, terrorism itself will no doubt continue to afflict us as long as injustice does; nor will it be less inhuman until our civilization is.

Edmond Taylor is the author of The Fall of the Dynasties *and two volumes of memoirs,* Richer by Asia *and* Awakening from History. *His article "Camoëns and the Epic of the Lusiads" appeared in the Autumn, 1972, issue of* HORIZON.

"You Cannot Imagine How it Spoils One to Have Been A Child Prodigy"

Whether playing the rake or the monk
or the lover or the
pianoforte, Liszt was especially
fond of cadenzas

A debonair young aesthete, Liszt posed early in his career, in 1839, for this sketch by Ingres.

Even if he had never written a note, Franz Liszt would still have been one of the most fascinating figures of the romantic age. He would be remembered as a kind of beautiful buffoon: Liszt the incomparable pianist and irresistible lover; the elegant, long-haired *arriviste* from Hungary who swept assorted countesses off their feet, not to mention Lola Montez and Marie Duplessis, *la dame aux camélias.* The astonishing thing is that he could do all this and still manage to compose music, vast quantities of it, thereby leading one of the most productive and, at the same time, most dissolute lives of the century.

Listening to Liszt's music, you sense that his life was spent modulating from the sublime to the ridiculous and back again. Sometimes it gallops along in a pianistic frenzy, as though its only ambition were to display the ten most acrobatic fingers in the whole world. At other times it will hold you spellbound, not with the choreography of the fingers but with the dance of ideas and audacity of sounds. There is a melancholy grandeur that stamps his *Sonetti del Petrarca,* for example, as the work of a very great composer, perhaps the greatest of his time.

His was a long and crowded career that encompassed just about everything that was happening on the musical scene. He received a kiss from Beethoven as a boy, helped Berlioz to his first success and Rossini to his last, befriended Mendelssohn and Schumann, stood as sponsor to Chopin, championed the cause of Wagner, taught Smetana and MacDowell, discovered Borodin and Mussorgsky, and prepared the way for Debussy. His life, from 1811 to 1886, was a perpetual series of experiments—in matters pertaining to the flesh as well as the spirit; to music, women, and the state of his soul. It was his personal version of the century's great quest for the absolute romantic experience. "You cannot expect from an artist that he should forego love in any form whatever," he once wrote to a woman who was trying to hold him back, "neither the sort that moves the senses and emotions, nor the ascetic and mystical forms of love."

In later years he took minor orders in the Catholic Church and wore a cassock, as though to disavow the follies of his youth, but even then the scandalous rumors that were told about his private life could hardly keep pace with the facts. Women adored him, and he, in turn, was terribly dependent on them; according to one of his mistresses, "he can do nothing great without a woman's quiet but constant, gentle, mild and devoted company." And the more the better: "Indeed, he must have several women around him, just as he needs many instruments in his orchestra, and many rich tone colors." Men, understandably, tended to distrust his motives. To some people he was a model of generosity; to others a monster of vanity. In his own estimation he was "half-gypsy, half-Franciscan." He liked to believe that the Liszt family was descended from the Hungarian nobility, and spoke of "remaining a Hungarian in heart and mind from the cradle to the grave," but he never learned to speak Hungarian. He fathered several children without acquiring a single wife, and lived in innumerable houses without ever having a permanent home. When Berlioz called him the *vagabond infatigable,* he was speaking metaphorically as well as geographically. But this rootlessness also served to prevent his music from becoming Germanic and conventional. He abolished the frontiers of musical Europe just as he eliminated the old division of labor between left-hand bass and right-hand treble on the piano, so that his two hands could range the full length of the keyboard, ready to strike singly or in pairs, like two panthers on the prowl.

None of this is altogether surprising in a man born on the borderline between nations and epochs. The village of Raiding (now Dobóján), where Liszt was born on October 22, 1811, belonged to the vast feudal domains of the Esterházy princes of Hungary, but the Austrian frontier runs just to the north, and Vienna is only sixty miles away. Both parents descended from peasant families. The father, Adam Liszt, was a Hungarian—one of twenty-six children—who worked as an estate manager for the Esterházys. The mother, née Anna Lager, came from German-Austrian stock, and the couple spoke German at home. Adam was an enthusiastic amateur pianist and string player. "Inwardly dissatisfied by his own wasted life, he was all the more anxious to give his son the advantages he had never known," says the biographical sketch that Liszt and Ludwig Rellstab produced in 1842.

Ambitious fathers—as Leopold Mozart had demonstrated—make efficient drillmasters. The boy was six when his musical talent was discovered, and after three years of lessons with his father he was ready to make his concert debut. Soon afterward Adam gave up his job to take the boy to Vienna for study, then on to Paris to be exhibited as a child prodigy. Fashionable ladies in the Faubourg Saint-Germain fussed over "Le petit Litz," and the Paris correspondent of the London *Observer* reported that, since Mozart, "the musical world has certainly witnessed nothing so surprising as young Leist."

"You cannot imagine how it spoils one to have been a child prodigy," Liszt said in later years, yet for him it was an emotionally deprived childhood. Adam Liszt had sent his wife back to Austria, ostensibly because traveling would be too strenuous for her, but chiefly because he wanted to make a man of his son without feminine interference. Franz's inevitable revolt against his father's petty tyranny took the form of religious fantasies. He announced his intention of becoming a monk, and "poured out his young soul in ardent prayers that lasted for hours." A course of baths at Boulogne was supposed to cure these disconcerting tendencies, but the treatment was cut short by Adam's sudden death in August, 1827. "On his deathbed in Boulogne my father told me that I had a good heart and mind, but that he feared that women would dominate me and confuse my life. This was a curious premonition, for at sixteen I still had no idea of what a woman was . . . "

Anna Liszt came to Paris to keep house for her son, who now earned a living for them both as a piano teacher to the nobility. Unused to the ways of the fashionable world, she was utterly powerless to prevent her husband's prophecy from being speedily fulfilled. The saga of Liszt as a lover begins, uncharacteristically, with a debacle: he fell in love with the most attractive of his pupils, the seventeen-year-old Countess Caroline de Saint-Cricq, but her father, finance minister to Charles X, refused to hear of it. The lessons were interrupted in mid-chord, and Caroline was bundled off to a suitable husband in the south of France.

It was the heyday of Byronic love, and Liszt suffered accordingly. For months he shut himself off from the world "to engage in a mighty battle with the soul." When he re-emerged he had become a confirmed believer in Saint-Simonism—a kind of pre-Marxian socialism calling for the abolition of poverty and privilege (after which countesses would be allowed to marry piano players). When the July Revolution broke out in 1830, Liszt was inspired to write a *Symphonie Révolutionnaire,* only to find himself co-opted by the accession of Louis Philippe.

More important for his art were the encounters with Berlioz, Paganini, and Chopin during the years that followed. Liszt attended the première of the *Symphonie Fantastique* in December, 1830, "and excited general attention by his applause and enthusiasm," as Berlioz notes in his memoirs. "We were strongly attracted to each other, and our friendship has increased in warmth and depth ever since." Liszt's dazzling piano transcription of the *Fantastique* did more than anything else to establish its European reputation, and he paid the expenses of publishing it out of his own pocket. The poet Heinrich Heine writes of hearing him play part of it at a

soiree in the fashionable Chausée d'Antin: "Liszt allowed himself to be pulled over to the piano, pushed his hair back over his genius's brow, and then engaged in one of his most brilliant battles ... He played that marvelous piece, the *March to the Scaffold* by Berlioz ... the whole room was filled with pale faces, heaving bosoms, light breathing during pauses, and finally furious applause. The ladies always act intoxicated when Liszt has played something for them."

Niccolò Paganini made his triumphal entry into Paris in March, 1831, looking like a "vampire with a violin," as Heine wrote. When he played, "it was as if all creation obeyed his sounds." There were people in the audience who claimed to have seen the devil standing at his elbow. The lesson in showmanship—how to make virtuosity sound diabolic—was not lost on Liszt. "What a man, what a violinist, what an artist!" he wrote. "What suffering, misery, torture in those four strings!" Fascinated by the hard, wiry sound of Paganini's *Caprices,* he used them as the basis of six breathtaking bravura studies of his own, the *Paganini Études.* With these and the twelve aptly named *Études of Transcendental Execution* he transformed the whole art of piano playing. The fierce onrush of trills, skips, and runs, the sudden blows and stormy flourishes, shatter the last vestiges of classical symmetry in keyboard music. In Liszt's hands (which were very narrow, "with long and slender fingers that look as if they had twice as many joints as other people's") the piano becomes a surrogate symphony orchestra. "In the compass of its octaves it covers the entire range of an orchestra," he explained, "and the ten

fingers of one man are sufficient to reproduce all the harmonies which can be reproduced by an ensemble of a hundred musicians ... "

But it was Chopin who taught him the value of understatement; of all his contemporaries it was Chopin he most admired and tried hardest to imitate. In

the course of their friendship they took turns inspiring and annoying each other. Liszt was a superb mimic at the piano: one evening, playing in a darkened room at George Sand's country house, he tricked their closest friends into believing that it was the poetic Chopin, not the fiery Liszt, who was improvising for them. To prove another point, he played the same Chopin étude six times in a row, each time with a different set of shadings and tone colors. "I would like to steal from him the way to play my own Etudes," Chopin conceded, but he was irritated by Liszt's habit of taking liberties with his music.

In 1833, when he was twenty-two, Liszt met the "river nymph" with whom he was to embark on the great romantic adventure of his life. The Countess Marie d'Agoult was then twenty-eight, the mother of two girls, and the wife of an ex-colonel fifteen years her senior. Blonde and blue-eyed, she was said to be "six inches of ice over twenty feet of lava." Liszt made music to her, and spoke of art and philosophy. "As I listened to this young magician," she writes in her memoirs, "his vibrant words opened my mind to the infinite, now dazzling, now sombre, but always changing, into which my thoughts dived and were lost."

For more than a year they carried on a precarious clandestine affair.

The crisis came when Marie's older daughter died; some months later she realized that she was going to have Liszt's child. Elopement seemed the only honorable solution. When they ran away to Switzerland in the spring of 1835, leaving her surviving child at home, she saw herself as a "chosen one, destined as an offering for the salvation of this divine genius," while he was confident that she would "make something or someone out of me." Traveling through the Alps, and later through Italy, Liszt began setting some of his landscape impressions to music and ended by composing the magnificent series of mood pieces that were pub-

lished as *Années de Pèlerinage (Years of Pilgrimage).* Here the tone becomes muted and introspective; the technical devices he developed for his bravura études are employed, no longer as ends in themselves, but as a means of expressing "the confidential secrets of the soul" with new depth and intensity.

Marie d'Agoult had "martyred" herself on Liszt's account. Having burned her bridges to Parisian society, she hoped to keep him to herself in some secluded spot where she could play the role of doorkeeper, muse, and acolyte. That seemed reasonable enough, especially since Liszt himself always spoke of renouncing the world, of seeking "impenetrable solitude for his soul." It was, indeed, something of a leitmotif recurring at every stage of his career. In 1836 he told Marie that he was "tired of humanity and its hubbub. I desire only a little repose." In 1846 he resolved to "stop fluttering about." In 1868 he spoke of "living out my days in some unknown corner, working steadily,"

ILLUSTRATIONS FROM Berühmte Geigen 1800

and in 1877 of "settling down in some place, whether village or city, to work away there in peace until my last day." These were, of course, in the nature of New Year's resolutions. The truth of the matter was that he only came to life when he had an audience. After three years of living in self-imposed isolation on Marie's terms, he returned to the life of a traveling virtuoso.

For several more years he kept up appearances of sorts by spending the summers with Marie and their three children, Blandine, Daniel, and Cosima (one day to become the second wife of Richard Wagner), but the threads that held them together finally snapped.

During his vagabond epoch Liszt covered Europe from one end to the other, often in a horse-drawn *Reisewagen* that served as a salon by day and a bedroom by night. His tours took him to Spain and Portugal as well as to Russia and Scandinavia. In London he played for the young Queen Victoria, in Constantinople for the sultan of Turkey. He owned sixty waistcoats and acquired nearly as many medals as the Duke of

Wellington. In Hungary he received a jeweled ceremonial saber and was acclaimed a national hero; in Berlin crowds lined the streets when he made his departure in an open carriage drawn by six white horses. In Prague he ran into Berlioz, and filled in as toastmaster at a banquet given in his friend's honor. Berlioz says that he spoke magnificently, but "he drank well, too . . . At two o'clock in the morning, Belloni [Liszt's secretary] and I were still in the street, trying to persuade him to wait till daylight for a duel which he insisted on fighting with a Bohemian who had drunk *better* than himself."

Liszt's concert was scheduled for noon the next day, and Berlioz began to grow alarmed. "He was still asleep at half-past eleven; at last they awoke him, he gets into his carriage, reaches the concert room, receives a triple volley of applause on his entrance, and plays better than I believe he had ever done . . ."

Eventually, at thirty-five, he had had enough of being a "puppet" to virtuosity and retired from the concert stage. Even so, his audience—and his need for one—would give him no rest. He continued to play in public, but only for charity and never for pay. He had fallen in love again, with a lady whose immense wealth and exalted rank were clearly incompatible with the gypsy life. Princess Carolyne Sayn-Wittgenstein, whom he had met in Kiev that spring, was a fascinating, but not at all frivolous woman of twenty-eight, well-read, widely traveled, and, like himself, a devout Catholic. She had a ten-year-old daughter, but was separated from her husband, a German prince in the service of the Russian czar. Hoping to obtain an annulment so that she could marry Liszt, they took up residence in the German Grand Duchy of Weimar, where he was appointed "Court Kapellmeister Extraordinary."

It was already the late afternoon of romanticism, and Liszt's music now acquired some of the pomposity that is so painfully prevalent in German music at

mid-century. For this, the princess must be held at least partially responsible. She thought him too prone to waste time on trifles and kept him hard at work composing music on suitably philosophical subjects. While he was busy writing scores at one end of their Wei-

mar studio, she sat at her desk at the other end of the room, writing essays and keeping an eye on him.

Nearly all of Liszt's orchestral works belong to the Weimar epoch: the *Faust* and *Dante* symphonies; the two piano concertos, and no less than thirteen symphonic poems, including *Mazeppa, Hamlet,* and *Les Préludes.* Much of this rings rather hollow on the modern ear, but Liszt is never less than fascinating, even when he insists on being pretentious, if only because every work involves so many new ideas and experiments in harmony and tone color. Having treated the piano like an orchestra, he now treats the orchestra like a piano, so that his symphonic poems sound like arrangements of some vast keyboard improvisation. At first he knew so little about orchestration that he had to have an assistant help him with the scoring, but one of Weimar's advantages was that Liszt could try out his symphonic works with the local opera-house orchestra before sending them off to be engraved. After some years of practical experience as a conductor, he developed an orchestral palette comparable to that of Berlioz; Ravel, the greatest of modern orchestrators, praised his "dazzling orchestra, of a sonority at once powerful and light."

The town of Weimar then had a population of only about twelve thousand, but under Liszt's aegis its opera house became a proving ground for all the avant-garde music of Europe. Berlioz came here for the German premières of some of his most important works, as well as the first effective revival of *Benvenuto Cellini.* Wagner's *Tannhäuser,* which other conductors had refused to touch, made its ap-

A Hungarian artist impaled Liszt in 1873 with these caricatures of the great man—the "Sun King of the Piano"—playing his own works with customary brio.

pearance in 1849, and shortly afterward Wagner himself arrived in Weimar, a fugitive from the Dresden police after the abortive Saxon revolution. Liszt helped smuggle him into Switzerland with funds provided by the princess. A year later, though Wagner was still on the wanted list, *Lohengrin* had its world première under Liszt's direction. Convinced that the "glorious" Wagner would grow "more and more glorious still," he would have gone on to produce the *Ring of the Nibelung* if Grand Duke Charles Alexander had not cut his budget. Wagner, for his part, accepted Liszt's loans as willingly as he learned from his scores, or, as Debussy put it, he "conscientiously plagiarized" from Liszt, "who met him with nothing but a kindly smile of acquiescence."

The young Czech composer Bedřich Smetana thought that Liszt at Weimar was like "a King of Music with a court of chosen artists from every part of the world." Only the townspeople of Weimar took a less respectful view of their distinguished visitor, and regularly hissed his productions at the theatre. It was his morality rather than his art that offended them, and his mistress had been seen smoking cigars in public. Feeling "systematically badgered from within and without," Liszt resigned his post in 1858 and followed the princess to Rome.

They still had hopes of getting married. After years of delicate negotiations (and payment of a seventy-thousand-ruble bribe), she had obtained a divorce from the Russian authorities and lacked only the Vatican's consent to her remarriage. For a time it looked as though no objections would be raised. Arrangements were actually made for them to be married on his fiftieth birthday, October 22, 1861. But on the eve of the wedding, just as the church was being decked with flowers, Pope Pius IX ordered a postponement so that the case could be reviewed.

The princess regarded this as a sign from heaven to abandon her worldly ambitions and devote herself to intellectual pursuits. Shutting herself into a vast Roman apartment to which fresh air was never admitted, she wrote a dozen books of spiritual guidance for "ladies of the world," and then plunged into her twenty-four-volume magnum opus, *Causes intérieures de la faiblesse extérieure de l'Église (Inner Causes of the Outward Weakness of the Church)*. The whole project became an embarrassment and a tribulation to Liszt, who would have preferred her to leave such questions to the theologians. "With my admiration is mixed a little stupefaction and even—dare I say it?—fear," he wrote to her after receiving the first two volumes, totaling 1,277 pages. But he need not have worried: eventually, all twenty-four volumes were placed on the Index Expurgatorius and never heard from again.

Liszt could not have been altogether disappointed to find himself past fifty and still unmarried. "The *allegro con brio* of his life lay behind him," as a friend noted, and now he longed once more for a quiet retreat. Friends at the Vatican arranged for him to stay at a cloistered apartment in the monastery of Santa Maria del Rosario, on the Monte Mario, attended only by a servant and a priest who said mass every morning. Yet in the evenings he still went out into Roman society, pursued by titled ladies who wanted to hear him play the piano. As a newly created knight of the Austrian order of the Iron Crown, he now had a title of sorts and could have himself announced as "Kammerherr von Liszt."

In 1865 he was received into the first four of the seven degrees of the Franciscan order: those of doorkeeper, reader, acolyte, and exorcist. Henceforth he wore the cassock and clerical collar and was known as the Abbé Liszt, but again these were honorary distinctions. He was not a priest and could neither celebrate mass nor hear confession; but he was free to leave the order to marry if he chose. "People pay me the compliment of saying that I wear my cassock as though I had worn it all my life," he wrote to a friend. A more skeptical observer, seeing Liszt in his new robes, thought he resembled "Mephistopheles disguised as an Abbé. Such is the end of Lovelace."

Though he wrote a great deal of church music during the 1860's, there was not enough musical activity in Rome to keep him permanently occupied. Then the voyages began again. He was persuaded to spend part of each year teaching in Germany and Hungary, and this *"vie trifurquée"* necessitated a constant round of journeys in "that vast and burdensome triangle, Pesth, Weimar, Rome." For seventeen years he regularly spent the spring in Weimar teaching a flock of young pianists, among whom were some rather less gifted girls whom he never had the heart to turn away. The cassock detracted nothing from his sex appeal: "women still go perfectly crazy over him," a pupil noted.

It was just as well that he had not taken a vow of chastity. *"J'ai un triste conception de l'amour,"* he liked to say, but that did not prevent him from adding to his store of experiences. When he was already sixty he had a nerve-racking escapade with the "Cossack Countess," Olga Janina, afterward the author of an embarrassingly detailed exposé, which, as a woman scorned, she sent to all his important friends. Olga, a wild Ukrainian horsewoman in her early twenties, fell in love first with Liszt's music, then with the man himself. Enrolling as one of his pupils in Rome, she resolved, "He shall be mine or I will kill him!" He surrendered to her without much of a struggle, in an apartment at the Villa d'Este that a cardinal had placed at his disposal. The next day, as Liszt slept, it struck her that he might have regrets, that thoughts of penitence would take him from her. Armed with a poisoned dagger, she braced herself for the awakening:

One tiny puncture and he was mine to all eternity, for we would lie under the same winding sheet in the same tomb. I held the dagger in . . . my hand and waited for his first word. It was one of love. He was saved.

She accompanied him to Weimar, then to Budapest, though her homicidal temperament and his world-weariness made an explosive mixture. In the autumn of 1871, after more threats of poison and pistols, she left him.

Liszt's attitude to music had, by then, entered its last and most astonishing phase. He still spoke of the "sustained sublimity" of Richard Wagner (who had recently become his son-in-law). But what he called "fat sounds"—*obésités polyphones*—were beginning to get on his nerves. "Germany is full of composers," he complained. "I am lost in a sea of music which threatens entirely to submerge me, but Heavens, how insipid it all is, not one living idea!" His great discovery of the 1870's was the *moguchaya kuchka,* or "Mighty Five," of Russian music: Mussorgsky, Borodin, Rimsky-Korsakov, Balakirev, and Cui. Drawn from the limitless reservoir of Russian folk songs, their modal music with its harsh dissonances proved to be a potent antidote to the emollient style of the Wagnerians. Liszt let them know how delighted he was that they had "brought something new into music," and warned them against falling under German influences. "You Russian composers are indispensable to us," he told Borodin when he visited Weimar. "The future belongs to you, while here I see nothing but lifeless stagnation all about." And yet the great temple to the "music of the future" built by his son-in-law at Bayreuth was less than eighty miles away!

In his own music—the whole fascinating body of work known to connoisseurs as "late Liszt"—he had turned equally modal and dissonant, but in his own fashion. Gone is the red plush of the Carolyne years; every pianistic ornament is stripped away; the harmonies range from stark open fifths to the most complex polytonal chords. The titles suggest that his mood was one of increasing melancholy: *Evil Star, Gray Clouds, Farewell, Abandoned, Forgotten Waltzes, Preludio Funebre, Via Crucis, Csárdás Macabre,* and *From*

Donning the habit of a Franciscan abbé, but avoiding chastity, Liszt apportioned his last years between women and composing music.

the Cradle to the Grave, his last tone poem. In 1882, shortly before Wagner's death in Venice, he composed the very somber *Funeral Gondola*—"as though," he said, "it was a presentiment." The one bright spot is the *Christmas Tree Suite* that he wrote for his grandchildren; its pieces are short and utterly simple, but as Busoni said, they reflect "that ultimate naiveté which is the fruit of all experience."

In these final works he prophesied much of what the twentieth century was to bring: Debussy's scales, Stravinsky's chords, Bartók's rhythms. Considered too "bizarre" to be published, many of them remained in manuscript until long after Liszt's death. Both friends and disciples were embarrassed by them. For Wagner, late Liszt was "the illustration of a sinking world" and "childish play with intervals." Even his best Weimar pupils were afraid of what these pieces represented. "Is one allowed to write such a thing?" asked August Göllerich about the dissonant *Csárdás Macabre.* "Is one allowed to listen to it?" Perhaps he realized subconsciously that a work like this symbolized a major turning point in cultural affairs—the shift of interest and influence from the center to the periphery of European music.

Liszt himself was past caring what people thought of it. His motto had become *Wir können warten* (We can wait). "I have to accustom myself to treating my music with a sort of systematic disregard and passive resignation," he told a friend. "The fact is that 'Monsieur Litz' is welcome everywhere when he shows himself at the piano—especially when he has made a career of doing the opposite. But they will not let him think and compose his own way . . . They may be right, but . . . I am filled with the spirit of resistance and determined to follow my own path to the end without pampering or deceiving myself."

In 1886, in preparation for his seventy-fifth birthday, Liszt visited Paris and London on a "Jubilee Tour." He heard his music at the Crystal Palace, dined with the Prince of Wales, and played for Queen Victoria again after an interval of more than forty-five years. He died on July 31 of that year at Bayreuth, during the festival of which he was then honorary president. Since his body was interred in precincts sacrosanct to Wagner, there was no Liszt memorial concert, not even a Requiem Mass for the Abbé. That the music of his last years might be worth performing was an idea totally foreign to Cosima Wagner, who thought her father had "renounced the achievements of a great art in order to imitate the gabble of priests."

It was left for Debussy, in the next generation, to discover the real significance of the avant-garde Liszt. Having labored under the delusion that Liszt wrote "disordered and feverish" music, Debussy was dumbfounded when he heard *Les jeux d'eaux à la Villa d'Este* for the first time; it proved to be one of the formative experiences of his musical life. And Bartók, after being put off by some of the bravura pieces, made a special study of the visionary Liszt and arrived at "the heart of the matter; it unlocked for me the true significance of this artist—for the future development of music I discovered in him a far greater genius than Wagner or Strauss." Perhaps it was the last of Liszt for which the first was made.

THE LAST
TIGER HUNT

Swift and ferocious, the tiger once held man at bay. In one of the earliest depictions of a tiger—an ancient seal from Mohenjo-Daro—Homo sapiens is up a tree. Opposite, in what may be one of the last views of a tiger in the wild, the cat is at bay.

Despite his legendary strength and ferocity,
the true king of beasts and
"most beautiful creature ever evolved"
is being systematically
eradicated by another animal as mobile and
adaptable as he is: man

By FRANKLIN RUSSELL

The approach of the tiger, no matter how silently and stealthily the big cat moves, sends alarm tremors running through jungle and forest, meadow and thicket. The harsh cries of jungle babblers and the screams of red-wattled lapwings warn of approaching death. In the open woodlands of central India, the ringing barks of sambar deer send the tiger-warning onward for half a mile. On the scrub plains of Rajasthan, blackbucks leap vertically, four legs held stiffly together, as their hoofs strum the ground in a signal to all who fear the approach of the cat. The gaur, India's massive, high-shouldered cattle, growl like dogs and trumpet tiger-danger in the forested hill country. Everywhere, monkeys cry, chatter, shriek, their alarms picked up by distant birds and transmitted through the forest. The peacock's vaguely human scream, hollow in the dim, early morning light, warns of tiger. It is all very disquieting; the presence of the tiger is heavy in the air.

Today, this unseen presence haunts more than India. The magnificent cat is retreating steadily toward extinction, perhaps fewer than two thousand of them remaining in India, compared with the estimated quarter of a million who roamed Asia one hundred and fifty years ago. The tiger is a reproach not only to Indians but to all humanity, forcing us to consider whether the cost of human progress must be the destruction of the unique and the beautiful.

What is most affecting, though—at least to me—is that the tiger is slipping through our fingers before anything much is known about him, as if we were destroying unpublished Shakespeare manuscripts while the poet lay dying. Before I went to India, I read the so-called literature of the tiger by such experts as Jim Corbett (*Man-eaters of Kumaon*) and A. Locke (*The Tigers of Trengganu*), and various other writers who have dealt with "man-eaters" and "jungle killers." But most tiger books consist of one anecdote disguised in a multitude of forms: how to get a bullet

A cacophony of shouts, drumming, and slashing swords drives a tiger toward the shooters in this late-

into a tiger's brain. Only one man, George B. Schaller, an American behavioral scientist, has published a careful work (*The Deer and the Tiger*) on the animal, and the Indian wildlife scientist K. Sankhala has recently completed a tiger life-study. Schaller has said that his work could only be a preliminary to the "desperately needed" Indian wildlife studies of the future.

The tiger remains an enigma inside the Indian paradox, in no way resembling the lion, his close relative. You can breakfast in New York on Monday and be looking at a wild African lion on

Tuesday. But you can arrive in Bombay, as I did, and be told by natural-history experts there that it might take you three or four weeks, if not months, to see a tiger. My pursuit of the tiger was like searching for a lost wilderness, or perhaps the lost innocence of man when a tiger skin on the hearth indicated a life well spent, not a crime against nature.

It was a journey into frustration because the tiger does not want to be seen by man, and I did not want to be an accessory to the habit of tethering live bait to attract him. Once, in the coastal forest south of Calcutta, I heard a tiger

eighteenth-century picture from Rajasthan. The marksman in the tree at left of center is probably Rajah Umed Singh, whose greatest love was the hunt.

grunting, a contemplative sound, as if he were preoccupied with some task. Next he woofed like a huge dog. A long silence followed, then came moans of exquisite feeling. My guide said, "Soon, we hear roaring." Instead, silence. One evening, in the foothills of the Himalayas, the air chill and silent, a flat *pok* sounded high in the hills. This was the voice of the tiger "pooking," a peculiar sound that resembles the warning call of the sambar, its function still a mystery. Sometimes, particularly after the monsoon has begun and the night air is damp and misty, a pair of tigers may

approach, apparently communicating. Their cries are inquiring *ahoo*'s, like distant ships hooting at each other, and the effect is electric, as if the cat had mastered a sound of man and transformed it into a wilderness voice.

The voice haunted me through thousands of miles of travel, made all the more evocative by the fact that I had not seen a tiger in the wild. I crossed the thornbush country of Gujarat and Rajasthan, and headed north across the Punjab into the uplands of Kashmir where the Himalayan foothills seal India off from the rest of Asia. A few

hundred tigers still survive there, but the only hint I got of their presence was an old pawprint and that strange *pok* in the night.

The tiger was once abundant in southern India, particularly in Mysore, a region that combines all the natural worlds of India—thick teak forests dripping moisture, blazing-hot thornbush country, open woods of broadleaved trees—but he had already gone from Mysore when I was there twenty years ago. He is gone from Orissa on the eastern coast as well, and survives only thinly in the Sundarbans, the grass jungles of West Bengal. I flew from Madhya Pradesh, in central India, across the Ganges toward the northern part of Uttar Pradesh, over the dense human occupation of the rich alluvial land flanking the river. The Gangetic basin is not only the genesis point of Indian civilization, it is also a barrier that no tiger can ever cross.

At Delhi, in south Uttar Pradesh, the zoo is famous for its breeding of tigers, including the fabled white tiger. A keeper there set a houseful of the big cats roaring for me and the sound was louder than a jet plane taking off. A nineteenth-century writer had described it as "the blaring of a thousand trombones," and my ears throbbed with the thunder of those fearsome, close-up voices. I began to understand why an Indian villager became anxious when he heard such a sound approaching from two miles away.

My search for the tiger was a journey through India and into the history of that country. The cat stands astride the history, first as a menace, then as a trophy, but always as an object of terror and reverence, a symbol of primeval power. Theatrically decorated in glowing reddish-bronze, the dark markings as distinctive as fingerprints, he is perhaps the most beautiful creature ever evolved on earth. No other cat except the leopard combines so perfectly the paradox of beauty and savagery. Since 1800 he has killed roughly 250,000 Indians, and no one has ever kept count of the millions of cattle, donkeys, sheep, goats, and domestic pigs he has eaten. Thousands of years ago he was a scourge in the land. A seal found in the remains of Mohenjo-Daro, a city that flourished five thousand years ago on the Indus, shows a man up a tree, a tiger lurking hungrily beneath.

The tiger influenced the settlement of India. Every Indian village had, and frequently still has, its wall of brush or stakes or thorns as defense against the cats. During the British imperial period, agriculture expanded, but the English often saw huge areas of farmland returning to jungle when the

farmers were driven back by that awful cry in the night and the deaths that followed it.

The tiger held his numbers stable, more or less, until the invention of the repeating rifle and the high-powered cartridge. Beginning about 1850, however, a steady slaughter of tigers, led by the inveterate English hunter and abetted by the aristocratic Indian sportsman, reduced the population to near oblivion. In the seven years before World War II, the Maharajah of Nepal and his guests disposed of nearly four hundred and fifty tigers. The Maharajah of Udaipur dropped at least one thousand tigers during his lifetime, while the Maharajah of Surguja had shot his way through colonialism, war, and democracy by April, 1965, for a grand total of eleven hundred and fifty tigers. In all, about one hundred thousand tigers have been killed between 1850 and today. Most of the great white hunters wrote books on their experiences, but few of them were able to reveal much natural history about their victims. "I'm afraid the tiger was studied mainly by men looking down the barrel of a rifle," says George Schaller. When K. Sankhala completed his intensive, continent-wide study of the tiger, he said that it had been extremely difficult to obtain modern or historical facts on the animal. "Everything about the tiger is controversial," he remarked, "and so is my study."

When I was a youngster, I knew an old and crippled Englishman who used to reminisce about his early days on an Indian tea plantation. "I thought I knew this animal," he would say, "but I never dreamed he would attack me in the house." The history of the tiger is punctuated by such statements. My English friend could not accept the reality of those great jaws filling his bedroom window.

As I traveled in India, growing more and more doubtful about ever seeing a tiger in the wild, I slowly realized that between the tiger hunter and his prey

lies India itself. The country has never been glamorized as Africa has been, and it is a nation a good deal harder to fathom than any part of Africa.

Hollywood cameramen head for Nairobi, not Delhi. There are no mass-media tales about pet tigers padding off to find their fortunes in the jungle. Instead, there are plenty of stories of the cruelties, the dangers, the dread of tigers. There is a pussycat atmosphere prevailing in lion literature, but the tiger represents the sinister, "the embodiment of devilish cruelty, of hate and savagery incarnate," in nineteenth-century hyperbole.

I peered into thickets and wandered the banks of meandering rivers and climbed into hills, but instead of tigers I found Indians. It is a marvel that the tiger has survived at all under the superabundance of humanity. In sweating jungles, at the icy fringes of the Himalayas, there is always an Indian. He occupies almost every available inch of his country. I drove through scores of villages, each covering about a square mile, each with its huts surrounded by fields of grass and crops. When the villagers are not working their main crop, usually rice planted in the monsoon and harvested toward the end of the year, they are wandering far in search of extra food. Their cattle and buffalo, which graze and browse freely in most forests, cannot feed them adequately. So they poach deer, snare birds, poison streams for fish, search seasonally for roots, mushrooms, any wild fruit. Nothing is missed by these gatherers. When they are not looking for food, they are cutting ungrazed or unburned grass for thatch, or slashing down bamboo to mix with mud for hut walls. "We have parks and sanctuaries," one Indian park official told me ruefully, "but barbed wire and armed guards cannot stop these people from doing what they've been doing for centuries."

The tiger cannot now get beyond the reach of people. In Rajasthan, villagers once united in sweeps through their thornbush thickets, slaughtering all the tiger cubs they could find. The Naga, living along the border of Assam and Burma, mobilized up to five thousand people to hunt tigers killing their livestock, and drove them, guided by wooden palisades, toward ravines, rifles, muzzle-loaders. Nineteenth-century villagers might venerate the European hunter with a gaudy parade, or just as easily revile him for killing the one animal that kept the ferocious wild pig in check. Today, the killing goes on. During my stay there, I encountered eight Indians who had shot tigers, one man even boasting a bag of forty-five in fifteen years.

Every Indian has his tiger story. I bumped along a thousand miles of dusty road, tigerless, but absorbed an encyclopedia of tiger mythology. His strength is legendary, a fact acceptable to the ear but frightening if you are waiting for a tiger in the branches of a tree. A tiger can pick up a five-hundred-pound buffalo and drag it a mile to cover. One tiger is said to have jumped a vertical fifteen-foot bank with a one-hundred-and-fifty-pound carcass in his teeth. Strength and size combine to make the tiger unpredictable. The timid villager, hearing the softest sound in the black night, may never know whether it is a two-hundred-pound tigress stalking a chicken or a seven-hundred-pound male who could knock a house down with one blow in his search for a cow, or an Indian.

The apocryphal mixes with the factual. The European reaches forward, picks up his gin and tonic, and sees the tray and its bearer whisked out through a window by a lithe, striped body. A man and his wife leave their hut in Mysore to visit some friends a few steps away in the village. In a second the man is widowed and never sees his wife again. An official of the Delhi Zoo, C. L. Bhatia, describes how a big male tiger panicked his elephant while he was on a tiger-watching expedition, then leaped up and tried to claw Bhatia from his high perch. George Schaller, who walked alone and unarmed through central Indian forests, was charged by a

tigress, but because he, like many tiger experts, believes the tiger does not readily attack men, he did not flee. The tigress stopped and roared at him.

"Most of the stories about tiger savagery are exaggerated," says J. T. Daniel of the Bombay Natural History Society. "But it is difficult to find room for both the tiger and people, and it is true that the tiger has eaten many people." The record for one tiger is more than four hundred human victims.

Facts on the tiger may be deceptive and unreliable, but the tiger's adaptability is demonstrable. He is, of all cats, the most nearly omnivorous. He eats any deer or antelope, and the dainty, spotted chital, India's most common grazing animal, is his favorite. He attacks massive gaur, the ferocious wild pig (which sometimes kills him), bison, and the porcupine (which can cripple or kill him with spines in face and feet). He stalks birds, and grubs around in ponds and streams for frogs and crabs and fish. He eats snakes and bears, locusts and turtles, termites and nuts, berries and other fresh fruit.

If he appears savage, it is because he is the modern version of the saber-toothed cat, descended directly from the animal that dominated Asia during the early Pleistocene era. At that time the forebears of the modern tiger and lion divided up the Old World between them. The tiger took Asia and spread southeast into the islands of the Pacific, south and west into India. The lion spread from Europe into the Middle East and then moved into Africa, some of his kind reaching northern India.

In his primeval state the tiger prowled the slopes of Mount Ararat in eastern Turkey, and in China, before that country was wrecked by deforestation, he padded through poplar and oak, hunted the peninsula that leads to modern Hong Kong, prowled Manchurian woods of scrub oak, walnut, and birch. He climbed mountain slopes into cedar forests, hunted northern China where the temperatures dropped to thirty below. Six feet of snow did not stop him. Neither did the stifling humid-

ity of Malaya. He slid through Indian grass jungles where monsoon rains drove grass up fifteen feet and where ground temperatures reached one hundred and fifty degrees. He walked the thirteen-thousand-foot-high pass between Sikkim and Nepal.

The superb adaptability of the tiger means he is unpredictable, which is why so many stories about him are conflicting. In Maharashtra I was told he was totally solitary, but in Nepal he is reputedly a family creature. In Madhya Pradesh he is sometimes eaten by wild dogs, but in Siberia he is reported to eat wild dogs, and even wolves.

My search for the tiger was not merely an education in natural history, it was also the experience of living among Indians. They call themselves a nation of four hundred million individualists, and they are right. They smile at Western ideas (even if they are using them), laugh at their own laws, and belong to so many separate states, religions, castes, and beliefs that the authority of the central government at Delhi sits lightly on them. "It is difficult, in such an atmosphere," says K. Sankhala, "to give the tiger the protection he needs." The pleas of the prime minister, Indira Gandhi, for tiger protection probably carry more authority than a thousand laws.

I did not have to travel far in India to feel the agony of a nation still in transition from the independence gained in 1947. For the tiger, independence was a disaster. It began what George Schaller calls "a period of destruction that could almost be compared to the slaughter of the American prairies in the 1880's." Not only the tiger suffered, but all wildlife and all forests. Added to this, the distribution of antibiotics and shipments of food sent the population rocketing from two hundred and fifty million to four hundred and fifty million in twenty years.

But even before independence, India's wildlife was in poor shape. Measured from a median point of 1900, almost all

Hunted by men on elephants, a tiger leaps at its tormentors in a painting done by George Chinnery in northwest Bengal about 1810.

Indian wild creatures were in decline. The crackle of the colonial administrator's rifle echoed from one end of the subcontinent to the other. The great Indian rhinoceros, once the sport of royalty, was reduced to a few animals in scattered sanctuaries. The Indian lion, once common over much of the north, survives today in one small forest; little more than a hundred animals remain. The magnificent Kashmir stag was brought down to around two hundred creatures. The buffalo became rare, fewer than two thousand animals. In 1900, herds of thousands of barasingha were seen by travelers, but now fewer than four thousand of them still survive. The blackbuck, once almost equally common, is now near extinction. The gaur, the chital, and all the other antelope, deer, and grazing animals are

mere shadows of their former numbers.

In this new world the survival of the tiger is a kind of wildlife miracle. It is possible because he is largely solitary (occasionally and unaccountably gathering in groups), a creature of territory, but also capable of migrations of two or three hundred miles. Because he is almost totally a night creature, he can move without detection, and with very little natural cover, from one hunting ground to another. He breeds throughout the year and, unlike the lion, he is fecund, ready to breed at two years of age. A tigress could theoretically produce up to forty youngsters during an average fifteen-year life.

Before the coming of the British, the tiger moved fairly freely throughout the continent. This freedom to move kept him in touch, genetically, with tigers

everywhere, from eastern Siberia to Turkey. But one other creature was just as mobile. Everywhere I traveled, I kept stumbling over powerful reminders of the absent British. Of course, I was traveling routes used by the tiger hunters of yesterday, but their impact on India must have been extraordinary. They moved easily throughout India, aided by a network of resthouses that isolated them from the "verminous populace." Many of these buildings stand today and are still in use.

They are monuments to British determination. Some still have sahib pictures on the walls, faded sepia photographs of Fotheringhams, Lytton-Smythes, Fanshawes, the colonels and the generals, the Bengal Lancers and the Royal Marines. Their front porches still hold massive stone steps for mounting elephants, camels, and the ox-drawn wagons that moved British goods and administrators before the railroads were completed. I sipped lemonade where the great hunters of the past had slept; Lieutenant-General Sir Montagu Gilbert Gerard, K.S.C.I., C.B. (tigers, leopards, bears); General A. A. A. Kinloch, C.B. (rhinoceros); Captain A. G. Arbuthnot, R.F.A. (bison); F. O. Gadsen, Royal Indian Marines (fish); Lieutenant-Colonel Bairnsfather, 14th Bengal Lancers (small game); Major Nevile Taylor, 14th Bengal Lancers (polo, pigsticking, general hunting). And what certainty they felt about their place in that world. For them, India was measured in terms of whether it was lightly or heavily "shot over," the density of its forests, the presence of its fevers, the availability and quality of its bearers.

Sweltering in the heat myself (two hundred Indians died of it in one week while I was there), I had to concede that these Britishers were supermen. They hunted in the worst of the premonsoon heat (roughly March through June) when the vegetation was driest, the woodlands open, the tall grass fallen or burned. In temperatures consistently above one hundred, these nineteenth-century diehards slogged up hills and across scorching plains, marching three to five hundred miles in a typical sixty-day shoot. They carried the ten-pound Express rifle, nearly .600 caliber, flush-sighted, its two hundred grains of black powder firing a hollow bullet that disintegrated or mushroomed on impact, the blow so powerful that the tiger invariably dropped, stunned, on being hit anywhere. The hunter might also carry a Paradox, a seven-pound gun that fired a twelve-bore solid ball accurately about one hundred yards, good for quick-running shots in heavy forest.

The tiger hunter bought almost all his equipment in India (a 90 per cent saving in costs), much of his clothing from the Army and Navy stores in Bombay, his weaponry from English gunmakers in Calcutta. From England, he brought a good pattern of his Norfolk jacket and walking breeches and had a local

durzi, or tailor, copy it. He chose his cloth meticulously, preferring the British mills at Cawnpore or fabric from the Basel Mission at Cananore; he picked his gaiters for resistance to thorns and snakes, while his ankle boots were of soft sambar leather over thick, plaited cotton soles without heels. He carried Indian-manufactured knives because British steel was too hard to resharpen in remote places. His tent, from Muir Mills at Cawnpore, weighed about one hundred pounds, and he traveled to Allahabad to get his beds, tables, chairs, washstands, and canvas tubs. His chaguls, or porous leather or canvas bags for water (evaporation kept the water cool), were of the highest quality.

To hunt "fairly comfortably," he needed five camels, which could be hired for about ten rupees a month in northern and central India. He took a khidmatgar, or valet, a water carrier, a dhobi, or washerman, a sweeper, or gunbearer, and at least two grooms. Each man was paid twenty to eighty rupees a month and was responsible for feeding himself. If the hunter carried good guns, he could get into the field for about a thousand dollars. The actual shikar, or hunting, expenses would run about five dollars a day.

He got up at sunrise, galloped or walked to his next camp by eight o'clock, sent on his rifles perhaps another six miles to where he would begin beating, breakfasted at his camp, and rode out to beat and shoot until just before sunset. Then he came back to camp, took his bath, "arrayed himself in light flannels, and dined." He never drank water while he was out in the field, unless desperate, and he never drank liquor before sundown.

This was the purest form of tiger killing. Unhappily, it was not the most common. The real shikarist was bitingly critical of the aristocratic Indian, and British, hunters who drove tigers between phalanxes of elephants (the tormented tigers had been known to

kill the mahouts). When royalty went hunting—and George V of England was representative—he was aided by five hundred elephants provided by a local dignitary. The elephants formed a line and advanced, the royal party firing generally at any movement in the grass. King George and his men bagged thirty-nine tigers. This most luxurious form of hunting enabled the hunter to wear white drill and tennis shoes, to carry an umbrella against the sun and baskets of iced drinks under the seat of the howdah. There was no danger. The ladies came along. It was "an Oriental rather than English form of sport." Everything was shot: deer, buffalo, hyena, tiger, leopard. Scores of animals died in a good drive.

Contrary to safari talk, lion hunting was rarely dangerous, but tiger shooting was often risky, if only because the big cat is so hard to kill. By the time I had been a month in India, five men had told me identical anecdotes about standing firm while shooting a charging, wounded tiger. I smiled politely but remembered a British hunter, G. P. Sanderson, who, in 1870, was called to deal with a pair of Mysore tigers. Some villagers had surrounded the animals with nets in a thicket. Sanderson managed to get bullets into both tigers after five days of what you could call mouse-and-cat tactics. It took him ten days to drive them into the open, where he shot them. The weather was hot. The tigers had no water and had been seriously wounded for five days. But at their death, they were active and dangerous.

In all my searching, I could not accustom myself to the incongruity of the places reputed to hold tigers. In central India, in particular, the landscapes that have been preserved from the forester and the farmer look European. Kanha National Park, a small jewel of a sanctuary about ten hours' drive from the city of Nagpur, I could never envisage as tiger country. The close-cropped grass, the neat meadows flanked by quiet, shadowed woodlands, appeared to be a parkland on a ducal estate. Small groups of chital, sambar, and

Leading a procession of elephant-borne hunters, the Prince of Wales, one day to become Duke of Windsor, goes on a tiger shoot in Nepal in 1921.

barasingha browsed. I expected a gaitered gamekeeper to come striding into view or to see fox hunters bursting out of the trees. Instead, memories of the tranquillity of Essex and Somerset were dispelled by the monotonous yammer of the brain-fever bird.

This disparity between peaceful landscape and ferocious cat was even more noticeable in southern India before the tiger was wiped out there. Great park-like landscapes in Mysore sheltered the tiger, and winding rivers were shadowed by dense stands of beech. Chitals drank there in droves, and kingfishers darted flashes of color upstream. The voices of doves and toucans and gray junglefowl gave the landscape an idyllic serenity that is uniquely Indian. Serene, that was, except for the tiger. He was driven into narrowing net traps, the night bright with blazing torches, until he was caught in a thicket, nets all around him. Then about twenty men, accompanied by guardian spearmen, entered the netted thicket and macheted a wide path through it. The English hunter had a clear line of fire. When the tiger leaped from one side of the thicket to another, a .570 caliber soft-nosed bullet was on its way.

Before the discovery that an agricul-

tural insecticide, polydol, injected into the carcasses of dead animals, was a certain tiger killer, the Mysoreans used strychnine. The tiger usually vomited up the poisoned flesh quickly, but he also ingested large amounts of strychnine. His roars of agony kept entire villages in touch with his position for days afterward. Tigers were also killed in many kinds of traps, particularly those that crushed them under slabs of rock that fell when they tugged at goats tethered beneath. Pits bottomed with sharp stakes were everywhere. One maharajah built replicas of the cage-type mousetrap, which, baited with goats, were trundled into the forest on wheels. Sanderson designed a giant springtrap to catch tigers, so strong it took four men to open the jaws, but he never caught anything with it.

Travel in India, whether in pursuit of tigers or not, is richly unpredictable. My elderly European car broke down in passage across a shrunken river in central India. In the silence, broken only by the sound of the steaming radiator and the creak of the driver's door opening, a low rumbling froze the driver, half out of the car. A tiger's face

slowly materialized from a nearby thicket. I watched, just as rigid, the slow baring of the teeth, the stretching and pulling back of the lips, the trembling of the whiskers. The pupils of the animal's eyes were tiny, glittering; the ears swiveled back to reveal their dark backsides, starkly marked with two light spots, themselves like eyes. The spots leaped from the camouflaged head with startling clarity, and they may indeed be intended to intimidate. The growl, a richly liquid sound of compressed fury, came from so deep in the body that it sounded independent of the throat itself, a subterranean rumble that promised an earthquake. The growling rose, then shut off in a choked roar. The tiger disappeared, probably to return to hidden cubs.

Perhaps it was that tantalizing glimpse of the animal, or perhaps I was just exhausted by the futility of trying to see a tiger in "natural" surroundings, but I finally joined the tourist circuit. In Jabalpur, a central Indian city, I gave in to the pleadings of a demented, ingenious entrepreneur—let me call him Rahul—who promised to drive me "many miles toward the great forest of the tiger." There, he vowed, a special tiger-viewing would be arranged "with abso-

Powerful-looking even in death, the first jungle cat felled in the shoot lies at the feet of the smiling Prince, seen with his Anglo-Indian entourage.

lute certainty." The first of the monsoon rains had begun, that immense invasion of Indian Ocean water that smothers much of the country when the high pressure and heat of the drought collapse. "But we must hurry," Rahul encouraged.

I had nostalgic thoughts of the early English hunter making his leisurely way across India, attended by his bearers, as I was hurled across Madhya Pradesh at insane speeds, locked in a ramshackle, Indian-made Ambassador with broken windows and no brakes or muffler, the trunk full of iced beer, hard-boiled eggs, ham sandwiches, and soft drinks. The Indian government does not like tourists to travel this way, and with reason. For fifteen hours we hurtled through crowded villages, splashed through rivers, bumped through woods and meadows, until we came to a small lake in a valley. Again, the appearance of a park: the lake sparkling clear, a gorgeous peacock gliding across it streaming a long tail. White-clad figures darted among the trees around a skinny cow tethered to a tree.

This is, of course, the characteristic method of viewing—and indeed, shooting—the modern tiger. It is about the only device that will bring the big cat into view in a land where every square mile swarms with enemies. But there is no guarantee that the tiger will appear that night, or a week hence. And the tiger watcher on such an unofficial expedition pays for the cow whether or not it attracts the tiger. I must regretfully report that after six hours, when the tiger did arrive to the sound of the thump of a heavy body falling, it was anticlimactic. The headlights of the Ambassador blazed out to reveal, like an overexposed snapshot, a beautiful, lithe form straddling the shoulders of the cow. There really was not very much to see. Jaws gnawed clumsily at the cow's neck, just behind the head, and a crack sounded, like a branch breaking. "Break neck," hissed Rahul. "You see enough, now?"

For a moment I did not understand, but Rahul reached into the back seat and pulled out a heavy rifle. "Now," he whispered, eyes glittering, "we kill." This took me so much by surprise that he had the gun out the window before I could react. "Just a minute," I said, wondering how to stop him, "that's my tiger. You leave it alone."

"No, no," he half shouted. I was glad to see the tiger look toward the lights.

"Mine. *My* tiger." He tried to take aim again. The tiger's skin, of course, was worth a small fortune to Rahul, and I could hardly bargain for the tiger's life. So I pressed the horn. The shrill beep sent the tiger gliding away instantly. For a moment, I thought I would be shot.

Later, in Calcutta, I saw tiger skins for sale in shops, tiger skins piled up in warehouses with blood still congealed on their fur. "Plenty of skins," said the salesman. "We can supply fifty skins a month, if you like." It was then illegal to kill the tigers, but not illegal to trade the skins. At about the same moment, Guy Mountfort, an international conservationist, was speaking in Delhi as part of a nationwide save-the-tiger program. There was no mention of the Rahuls, of Madhya Pradesh, or of the skin salesmen of Calcutta. The tiger represents an aesthetic dilemma that faces us all. The solution to it will give no more information on tigers, as they retreat to make their last stand, but it may be a commentary on another animal's struggle to survive in his diminishing world.

*Besides tigers, Franklin Russell reports on animals of many another stripe, such as elephants (*HORIZON, *Winter, 1973).*

Flanked by their gunbearers, three Victorian sahibs display trophies of the hunt. In the nineteenth century, most tiger hunters in India were

at least sportsmen, but today the beasts are killed—illegally—for their pelts. On the entire subcontinent, only about two thousand survive.

MANNERISM

Aloof and elegant, the ideal Mannerist courtier appears in Niccolo dell' Abate's Portrait of a Gentleman with a Parrot, *opposite page. Beneath the polite façade lurks another Mannerist image, man the grotesque, revealed above by Giuseppe Arcimboldo in his* Allegory of Fire.

W hat manner

of -ism is Mannerism? A manner of

speaking among art

historians? An affront to taste?

Virtuosity triumphant?

Or an elaborate practical joke?

By J. H. ELLIOTT

"THE MADONNA WITH THE LONG NECK"

To the Mannerists the chief object of art was to display the artist's virtù—*his inventiveness, boldness, and facility. Since inventiveness meant creating forms never encountered in nature, Parmigianino endowed his long-necked Madonna, above, with an ideal, anatomically impossible sinuosity. Inventing ideal forms of ugliness was equally challenging to such Mannerists as Giulio Romano, who in 1534 adorned a Mantuan palace room with giants, below, who look like human rubble. Overcoming* difficoltè *like foreshortening was another sign of artistic virtuosity, and painters such as Hendrik Goltzius delighted in depicting the human body, opposite, from the most distorting angles.*

"THE FALL OF THE GIANTS"

Something very strange happened in the world of the visual arts during the sixteenth century. In its opening years, the golden age of the Italian High Renaissance, the arts seemed to attain perfection. Leonardo, Raphael, the young Michelangelo, had shown that there was nothing that the artist could not do. Surpassing even the artists and craftsmen of classical antiquity, they had captured for their generation the lineaments of the ideal world that existed beyond the world of appearances. Beauty, harmony, proportion—these were the supreme characteristics of the ideal world of the Renaissance, an orderly, rational world in which man himself, divinely endowed with power and wisdom, walked godlike and majestic.

But moving on a generation or so, what do we find? The repose and serenity of the High Renaissance are gone, to be replaced by restlessness and confusion. The calm, statuesque figures have become strangely elongated, their gestures extravagant, their limbs so contorted as to remind us less of men than of corkscrews. Where is the proportion? Where the order? Where, above all, as we look at those incredible vegetable portraits by Giuseppe Arcimboldo, is the *dignity* of man?

It is clear that something has happened. But what? The advent, say some art historians, of "Mannerism." The style of the Renaissance or the Baroque presents us with no great difficulty. We all have a rough general idea of what these descriptive labels imply, and can produce the names of a few artists to match. But Mannerism? Even the experts seem unable to agree on a short list of Mannerist painters. Parmigianino? Yes, almost certainly, along with Pontormo and Rosso Fiorentino. But what about Brueghel, or El Greco, or even Tintoretto? For some, they are quintessentially Mannerist. For others, they are automatically disqualified because they are too solid, or too spiritual, or simply too energetic.

This acute uncertainty about the identity of Mannerist artists merely reflects an acute uncertainty about the nature of Mannerism itself. The Italian word *maniera,* as used in the sixteenth century, meant style; and although sixteenth-century critics, like Vasari, had no notion of being in the presence of an international art style called Mannerism, they did recognize that certain painters tended to imitate the *maniera* of certain great masters of the Renaissance. Pre-eminent among these masters was that all-around genius, Michelangelo, who seemed to have broken away from many of the canons of Renaissance artistic theory in his later works, and to have thrown up a whole galaxy of visual hints for future generations. But is there really enough common ground among Michelangelo's successors—outside of a small group of artists in Rome and Florence in the years after 1520—to constitute a distinctive and clearly identifiable form of art? Indeed, did Mannerism as an international style ever exist? Or is it merely the convenient invention of modern art historians? When Kenneth Clark refers scathingly in his *Civilisation* to the art of the later sixteenth century, "which has recently and ominously come back into fashion under the catch-penny title of Mannerism," we are at least entitled to ask ourselves who is fooling whom.

Since one man's Mannerism is another man's solecism, the variety of explanations is hardly surprising. For some, it represents no more than a natural development of Renaissance ideals of beauty in the pursuit of a supreme artistic virtuosity. For others, it represents the deliberate rejection of those ideals—a brusque turning away from classical proportion and harmony. Certainly if one looks at Giulio Romano's incredible frescoes in the Sala dei Giganti of the Palazzo del Tè in Mantua—frescoes depicting the Titans being crushed beneath the weight of cascading rocks and shattered columns—it is not too much of a strain on the imagination to see them as symbolizing the destruction of the ordered world of the Renaissance in some cataclysmic upheaval.

But why should this have happened? Why should the generation of the 1520's and 1530's have rejected the values and spurned the achievements of its predecessor—if, indeed, it did? Perhaps this was no more than the perennial conflict of generations, with Michelangelo, as the grand old man of a dying generation, setting the pace for youth. Or perhaps the world of the Renaissance, with its firm standards and fixed values, was itself, like the world of Giulio Romano's Titans, in the process of violent disintegration. There was reason enough for the men of the 1520's to feel themselves as impotent as the Titans of old when confronted with the fury of the gods. The 1520's saw Luther's defiance of the pope and the dissolution of the traditional unity of Christendom; the Ottoman assault on Central Europe and the crushing defeat of the Christian forces at Mohács; and in Italy itself the seismic shock of 1527, when the armies of the Holy Roman Emperor Charles V ran wild and sacked the Eternal City. It would not be strange if contemporaries, reeling beneath these disasters, should have lost faith in a rational and coherent universe and begun to believe that the world was dissolving around them.

Such an interpretation looks doubly attractive to a later generation, living under the shadow of nuclear catastrophe. Nor is it an accident that the age of Mannerism appears to speak directly to our own age across the gulf of centuries. The resemblances seem in some respects almost painfully close—the breakdown of established values, the sense of insecurity and deep spiritual malaise, the febrile or reckless response. "Play it for kicks," writes Kenneth Clark, "that is the mannerist motto, and like all forms of indecency, it's irresistible." Can it be that we are faced, in Mannerism, with the art of alienation?

ICARUS

IXION

Ingenious attempts have been made to explain the Mannerist style as just that. Medieval Christendom, we are told, was a corporate society in which every man knew his proper place, and in which everything was seen in relation to a framework of fixed and eternal values, duly interpreted for mankind by a universal church. But in the fifteenth and sixteenth centuries this traditional system of thought and values was shattered beyond repair. The Copernican revolution destroyed the certainty of an earth-oriented Aristotelian universe. The rise of Protestantism promoted spiritual individualism; the rise of capitalism, economic individualism. Under the pressure of the new individualism, the corporate structure of society began to disintegrate. Personal relations were dehumanized. Man found himself ranged against man, Catholic against Protestant, class against class. Meanwhile, new structures arose—vast state bureaucracies, institutionalized churches, international financial networks and banking organizations. Confronted with the new, dehumanized system, men felt themselves alienated from the society that was arising around them, and deliberately began to opt out.

To interpret Mannerism as the product of alienation is surely an attempt by the twentieth century to remake the sixteenth in its own image. Under scrutiny, the evidence of alienation in the intensely hierarchical society of sixteenth-century Europe, with its patriarchal families, its kinship and clientage structures, its fraternities and guilds, appears to be remarkably thin. Even thinner is the evidence that Mannerism expresses

PHAETON

87

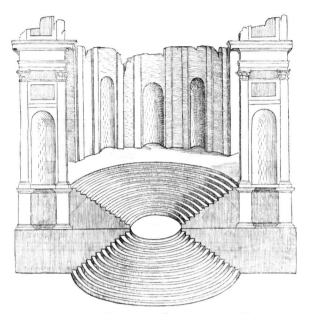

EXEDRA OF THE BELVEDERE COURTYARD, THE VATICAN

When Mannerist painters turned to architecture—as they often did—they treated buildings as three-dimensional paintings. The courtyard of the Uffizi, below, was designed by Giorgio Vasari, who sought to reproduce therein the pictorial effect of deep perspective recession. When built, the double staircase above, designed for the Vatican by Bramante, must have looked ambiguously two-dimensional. Reversing the order of illusion, Mannerists also adorned buildings with trompe-l'oeil *paintings of architecture. Giulio Romano's ceiling fresco, opposite, appears to be the room's actual dome, suggesting to the viewer that he needs only a ladder to join the Olympian gods.*

COURTYARD OF THE UFFIZI, FLORENCE

this alienation in literature and the arts. Can Mannerist art, with all its extravagance and absurdity, its sheer delight in the polished, the elegant, and the virtuoso, really sustain so portentous an explanation?

If we are to get any closer to this most stylish of styles, we must attempt to abandon our twentieth-century preconceptions and approach the sixteenth century on its own terms. In particular, we must look at the changing relationship between patron and artist as the status of the artist was itself transformed. For the medieval artist had been, above all, a craftsman—a manual worker whose identity tended to be merged into that of his guild. But the artistic theories of the Renaissance depicted the painter, the sculptor, the architect, in a new and distinctly more flattering light. The artist became a man who possessed a special insight into the ideal world, together with the capacity to bring that world alive for less privileged mortals. He was no longer a mere craftsman, but a figure more akin to the gentleman scholar—a man of culture, insight, and intellect, with a nobility of soul that was inevitably mirrored in his work.

When the artist rose in his own estimation and in that of society, he began to set a higher price on his services, and was less willing to be at the beck and call of a condescending patron. The new relationship was symbolized by the anxious attempts of that normally headstrong pope, Julius II, to calm down the equally irascible Michelangelo and induce him to return to Rome to paint the Sistine Chapel ceiling. Significantly, contemporaries knew Michelangelo as *il Divino:* the mere artist and the spiritual ruler of Christendom now met on equal terms. Once this had happened, the artist had effectively established his right to be pursued and courted for himself—as a man with unique gifts, reflecting his own unique character and abilities. The patron, for his part, was now at something of a disadvantage. He might have to move heaven and earth to acquire for his collection a work bearing the distinctive stamp of a Raphael or a Michelangelo.

To acquire for his collection . . . For the sixteenth century was preeminently the age of the collector. The discovery of new worlds overseas, and the increasingly close observation of nature, had brought home to European man the incredible variety and multiplicity of objects in the world he inhabited. Rich men who prided themselves on their taste and learning began to collect everything they could lay their hands on—gems, antique marbles and cameos, books and manuscripts, medals and bronzes, plants and animals, and every kind of outlandish artifact. Monarchs and private citizens created menageries and botanical gardens for their instruction and delight. Kings, cardinals, great statesmen, and public servants, like Cardinal de Granvelle, the minister of Charles V and then of Philip II, competed ferociously for masterpieces with which to furnish their private galleries.

Enthusiastic collectors were also frequently enterprising patrons, like members of the Farnese family, particularly Pope Paul III (1468–1549) and his nephew, Cardinal Alessandro Farnese (1520–89). Sooner or later most of the artistic celebrities of the age were drawn into the glittering orbit of their patronage—Michelangelo and Titian, El Greco and Cellini, Scipione Pulzone and Bartholomeus Spranger and Frederico Zuccari, the architects Giacomo da Vignola and Antonio da Sangallo the Younger. The eclectic Farnese family had room for them all in their splendid palaces, for their concern as collectors was less with any particular style

"TEMPLE OF HEAVEN," PALAZZO DEL TÈ, MANTUA

than it was with the acquisition of works of supreme virtuosity.

Virtuosity, to mid-sixteenth-century eyes, involved elegance and complexity, qualities cultivated by the earliest Mannerist painters of Rome and Florence. There was a similar aristocratic elegance about the international Gothic style of the fifteenth century, and this is one of the reasons why Italian Mannerism found such ready acceptance north of the Alps, where High Renaissance art had not established itself. The Renaissance traveled out of Italy in Mannerist disguise, frequently mingling on its arrival with native Gothic forms. Coming with all the prestige of its Italian origins, it permeated the art of the Netherlands and France and was eagerly adopted by patrons. For his palace at Fontainebleau, Francis I of France employed Italian artists to build Italianate galleries that would outshine those of his Italian rivals.

Artists naturally responded with delight to an environment of patronage in which they were expected to produce works that would display to the best advantage their own special vision and technical skills. They were expected to do their own thing —but to do it in ways that conformed to the mood and requirements of both their patrons and the times. Art still had a public face and indeed was deliberately exploited to proclaim the virtues of the ruling house, especially when the ruler had risen, like Cosimo I, grand duke of Tuscany, from comparative obscurity to sudden eminence. But at the same time it was also becoming a more intimate affair, as befitted the new age of the connoisseur.

This more private character of the relationship between patron and artist reflected the change from the urban society of the Renaissance to the princely civilization of the sixteenth century. The artist was now more likely to find himself working for the court than for the city. The new patrons, whether princes, nobles, churchmen, or bankers, had their own special tastes and requirements, which were different from those of town councils or guilds. They wanted their artists to be courtiers, and they wanted them to express in their paintings the ideals and the aspirations of a courtly society. The handbook of this society was a best seller of the sixteenth century: *The Book of the Courtier* by Baldessare Castiglione, himself a connoisseur of the arts.

In *The Courtier* Castiglione especially commended what he called "the peculiar quiet gravity of the Spaniards"; and if we look at those wonderful portraits painted by Bronzino for Cosimo I and his court, we can see how this "peculiar quiet gravity" had become the ideal of a whole generation. These cool, withdrawn figures, so elegant and so detached, never for a moment allow their guard to slip. Their faces are set, their stiff figures caught, in a timeless immobility. But Bronzino was a great enough artist to hint at the unease beneath those frozen surfaces. How Castiglione would have approved! "That may be said to be true art that appears not to be art; neither ought a man to put more diligence in anything than in covering it."

The art that conceals art—this was the real virtuosity, and the supreme ideal, of the Mannerist generation. And it seemed an ideal more capable of realization than for any generation preceding it. The technical inventiveness of fifteenth- and sixteenth-century Europeans gave them the beginnings of sovereignty over nature. Theirs was a civilization that was reaching out—in navigation, in astronomy, in science and technology— toward that supreme aspiration of man: the mastery of his own environment. The arts could hardly remain unaffected by this new technolog-

SKELETON

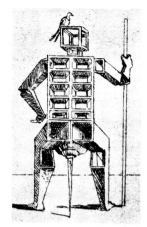

CUBISTIC MAN

MONSTER

GROTESQUES

As self-styled creators of meraviglie, *marvels, the Mannerists took delight in bizarre and shocking effects. They found them in macabre incongruities such as Hans Baldung-Grien's mating of the erotic and the ghoulish, opposite. They found them, too, in woodcuts of the flayed human body, at top, first published in Andreas Vesalius's anatomical treatise of 1543 and copied many times over. Sketches of allegedly natural freaks like a human-faced pig, creatures of whimsy such as Giovanni Braccelli's cubical man, whole breviaries of droll, quasi-human grotesques, poured from the workshops of sixteenth-century artists under the influence of one of Mannerism's central tenets—that, in the words of the Florentine poet Piero di Cosimo, "strangeness is a source both of grace and of art."*

"Cosimo I, Archduke of Tuscany," Vasari

Mannerism was a courtly art, commissioned by and designed for princely patrons. By promising "bizarre inventions never seen before," to quote a contemporary artist, Mannerists hoped to win the favor of the Medici patron Cosimo I (in Vasari's portrait, above, Benvenuto Cellini is seen looking over Cosimo's left shoulder); be asked by Francis I, below, to decorate the palace at Fontainebleau; or be invited to Prague to join the eccentric Holy Roman Emperor Rudolf II, opposite. Like the Mannerists themselves, such sixteenth-century patrons judged a work of art by the extent to which it appeared a marvel of virtuosity.

"Francis I," Jean Clouet

ical command. In painting, the Mannerists inherited from their predecessors the materials and the skills, the laws of perspective, the control of space and color, that enabled them to represent people and objects with extraordinary fidelity. In architecture, sculpture, and the lesser arts the same sense of command is apparent. Everywhere artists showed themselves possessed of an inventiveness, a craftsmanship, and, above all, a confidence that allowed them to shape and mold their materials to suit their own caprice.

Under the circumstances, it is not surprising that the sheer delight in craftsmanship should have been so pronounced a characteristic of sixteenth-century art. Benvenuto Cellini reveled in his own virtuosity, whether in setting diamonds or in making his famous salt cellar for the king of France. "I put a trident into the right hand of the figure that represented the sea, and in the left a bark of exquisite workmanship, which was to hold the salt. Under this figure were its four sea-horses . . . The earth I represented by a beautiful female figure holding a cornucopia in her hand, entirely naked, like the male figure . . . There were also four other figures of the four principal winds, the workmanship and enamel of which were elegant to the last degree."

The delight in virtuosity was everywhere—in the incredibly intricate settings of precious gems; in clocks and watches with ingenious mechanisms; in elaborate suits of armor (so unnecessary in the age of the no less elaborate gun). It was to be found indoors, in complicated chimney pieces and in twisting stairways. If, as Sir Francis Bacon was later to write, "all rising to great place is by a winding stair," it was the architects of the preceding generation who had seen to it that no palace or villa was without one. The virtuosity was to be found out-of-doors, too, in those superb sixteenth-century gardens where the visitor was surprised with every kind of contrivance and conceit, from the carved rock fantasies of the grotto to elaborate fountains and concealed jets of water that would suddenly soak him to the skin.

Artificiality abounded. And this, perhaps, was the root of the trouble. Life at court and in aristocratic households came to be conducted in a language that could be deciphered only by the initiated, since it consisted of private jokes and hidden meanings shared among patron and artist and a select circle of friends. In this world of emblems, epigrams, and hidden allusions, the manner all too frequently came to mean more than the matter. Man could not live indefinitely by virtuosity alone.

By the middle of the sixteenth century the mood was already beginning to change, and artists, as so often, were among the first to respond. Many of the supremely elegant artistic productions of the times were distinctly short on spiritual content. But it was precisely spiritual content that the new age of fierce religious partisanship was beginning to demand. There was too much paganism, too much permissiveness, too much sensualism and nudity, in the art of the first generation of the Mannerists. It was time for artists to be brought back to their proper duty—the deployment of their talents for the greater glory of God.

The tide was running strongly toward a new puritanism in the Roman Catholic Church when the council of church fathers, originally summoned to set the Church's own house in order in the face of Protestant attacks, reopened at Trent in January, 1562. The arts had come under grave suspicion as offenders against dignity, restraint, and decorum. There was even a move to suppress all harmonic music in church, for the complicated

"AUTUMN," UNKNOWN FOLLOWER OF ARCIMBOLDO

The so-called "vegetable portrait," above, was first made popular by Arcimboldo, court painter to Rudolf II. Many observers have noticed in the features of Arcimboldo's vegetable men a close likeness of the emperor, a lover of marvels who was delighted in equal measure with the Mannerist whimsies of Arcimboldo, the experiments of his court alchemists, the wizardry of his court astrologers, and his own collection of rare animals and curiosities.

polyphonic masses and motets in fashion at the time seemed less designed to express genuine religious emotion than to display the technical skill of the composer to the best advantage. Similar criticisms were levied against the modern style in painting, and even the "divine" Michelangelo came under censure for the naked limbs of his posturing nudes. The council took due note of the criticisms and formally pronounced. Sensuality and superfluous elegance in images and altarpieces were solemnly condemned. In tune with the spirit of the times, Pope Pius V saw to it that the nudes in Michelangelo's *Last Judgment* were decently adorned with drapery.

It is not surprising, then, that a new sobriety and sternness of purpose are to be found in the religious painting of the later sixteenth century. Older artists, like Bronzino, had to change their ways, while younger ones, like El Greco, found fresh springs of inspiration in the new religious climate. But this did not mean that Mannerist techniques had to be abandoned. Those corkscrew shapes, those elongated bodies, could be used, as Tintoretto and El Greco were to prove, to dissolve the earthly form of saints and martyrs and to infuse them with a strange, incandescent spirituality.

The generation of the early seventeenth century would evolve, in the Baroque, a more robust and energetic style, appropriate to an age of returning spiritual confidence. But the troubled years that followed the conclusion of the Council of Trent were for many a period of uncertainty and doubt. Revolt in the Netherlands; religious wars in France; widespread conflicts between Catholics and Protestants in a continent overshadowed by the power of Catholic Spain. How could any man who was not an extremist steer his course in such a perturbed and hazardous world?

"RUDOLF II," ADRIAEN DE VRIES

GROTTO, ORSINI GARDENS AT BOMARZO

To literary taste of the era—which was for tales of knights-errant, sorcerers, giants, and ogres—Mannerism provided an illustrated counterpart. In the gardens of palaces, Mannerists offered islands of enchantment to "ladies and cavalieri of the courts." They could enter a Roman garden, below, through a demon's mouth; walk into the jaws of Hell, above; and see, as in a fable come true, a giant turning into a mountain. The books of chivalry that drove Don Quixote mad gave to Mannerism a fine madness of its own.

DOORWAY, PALAZZO ZUCCARI AT ROME

One answer was to arm oneself, like Montaigne, with the weapons of irony and skepticism, and remain aloof from the battle. Another was to search the cosmos for hidden allusions, for the secret concordances of the stars and the planets that held the key to the reconciliation of mankind in some sublime religious synthesis.

Each of these reactions was, in its way, conducive to the survival of Mannerist forms in literature and the arts. If the elegant irony of the Mannerist style made it less and less appropriate for religious purposes, it remained well suited to the more secular needs of those who lived a life of refinement far removed from conflict. The private jokes, the recondite allusions, helped to perpetuate the illusion of detachment from a world that was tearing itself to pieces in religious frenzy. Faced with such a world there was an obvious answer: to cultivate one's curios.

But detachment was not the only answer. In a mental world where symbolism and the inner vision of the artist found themselves at a premium, it is no accident that Mannerist art should have enjoyed its final flowering at the very end of the sixteenth century, in the court of the emperor Rudolf II at Prague. This most enigmatic of the Hapsburgs, obsessed and melancholic, precariously treading a line between sanity and madness, expressed in his own person many of the aspirations and tensions of his age. Was he not the providentially chosen defender of a natural harmony that the extremists would destroy? Could not the study of art, astronomy, and magic yield universal truths? Shut away in his castle in Prague, he brooded on the secrets of the universe in the company of a few kindred spirits who had come from all over Europe, drawn by the magnet of his patronage and his strange reputation. There were alchemists and dabblers in the occult, like the learned Welsh astrologer and mathematician John Dee. There were the famous astronomers Johannes Kepler and Tycho Brahe. There were scholars and cranks and charlatans; and ingenious—if not very inspired—artists, like Bartholomeus Spranger from the Netherlands; and the Italian Giuseppe Arcimboldo, who was commissioned to seek out curiosities for the imperial collection.

It was a strange twilight world that these men inhabited, at once cosmopolitan and intensely private. And at the heart of it sat the emperor, whose mysterious personality posed as deep a riddle as any that he himself attempted to resolve. Patron of the arts and sciences, magician and recluse, he would spend hour upon hour shut away with his gems and curios, his superb cabinets of art treasures bought from all over Europe, or in the famous picture gallery where he gave full rein to his penchant for the allegoric and the erotic—Leda and the swan, Hercules and Omphale, Vulcan and Maia, old men making advances to coyly bashful girls.

What, if anything, did all this mean? The mystery remains that of Mannerism itself. Was it simply the elaborate private game of defeated men in retreat from the world? Was it an attempt to draw on the inner vision of the artist-magician, who alone could see through the multiple fragments of a shattered universe to the underlying harmony? Or was it no more than a confidence trick perpetrated on gullible patrons by artists of dazzling virtuosity? Just possibly it was all of these. If so, the paradox is at least permissible. There is, after all, nothing more serious than the really clever joke.

J. H. Elliott, Professor of History at King's College, London, is the author of Europe Divided: 1559–1598, *which deals with the Mannerist period.*

ILLUSTRATIONS CONTINUED OVERLEAF

"ALLEGORY OF THE APENNINES," VILLA DEMIDOFF AT PRATOLINO

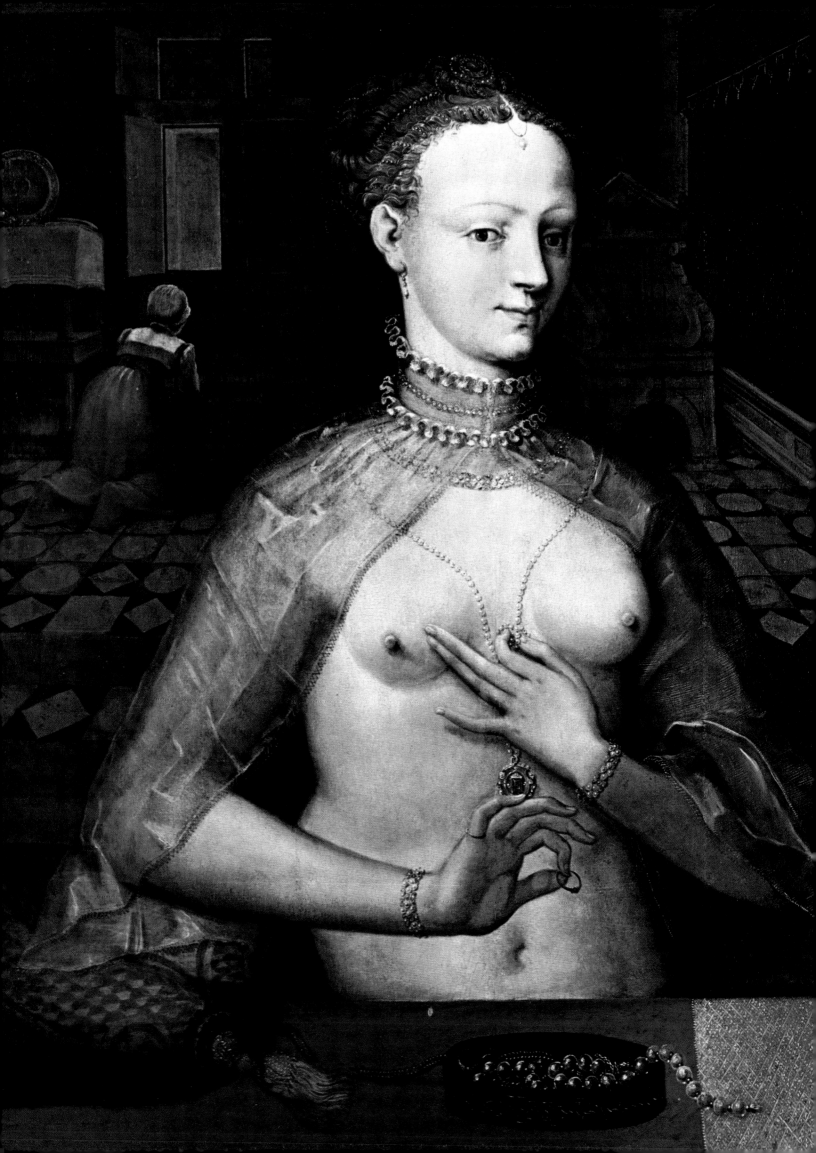

THE HUMAN BODY

NUDE, SISTINE CHAPEL CEILING

CUBISTIC FIGURES

To the Mannerists the most compelling of all subjects was the naked human body, which they rendered, however, as if the human form were beautiful only when it did not seem quite real. In making human beauty appear artificial, the Mannerists employed a number of devices, most of them discovered by their great hero, Michelangelo. They sought, for one thing, to give the human figure the appearance of sculpture, in imitation of Michelangelo's Sistine ceiling nudes, above. At Fontainebleau, there was a veritable mania for erotic paintings of naked women; yet the *Lady at Her Toilet,* at left—reputed to be the king of France's mistress, Diane de Poitiers—was carefully made to look like a figure of wax, as though fleshiness were too vulgar for beauty. Paradoxically, the Mannerists seemed to dematerialize the human body in the act of glorifying it, a tendency that culminated with Luca Cambiaso, who dispensed entirely with flesh and created cubistic figures, above. To make the human body appear a work of art, the Mannerists also depicted it in wonderfully twisted poses—another discovery of Michelangelo's—in which the very strain involved made the figure's elegance seem willful and affected. To render such twisted poses, known as the *figura serpentinata,* Mannerists endowed the human form with unnatural elasticity and a disproportionate length of limb, itself a Mannerist declaration: the artist and not nature created true beauty, even the beauty of the flesh.

OVERLEAF: The stylized human figure is seen in five celebrated Mannerist paintings, also reproduced in miniature below. They include Angelo Bronzino's *John the Baptist,* in which the saint is a beautiful fop. Bronzino's *Allegory of Venus, Cupid, Time, and Folly* is a scene of perverse Mannerist eroticism: an elderly lecher peeks at an incestuous embrace. *Moses Defending the Daughters of Jethro,* done around 1523, provided Rosso Fiorentino with his pretext for a favorite Mannerist scene—a turbulent tangle of naked, contorted bodies. In Bartholomeus Spranger's *Minerva Victorious over Ignorance* the goddess of wisdom is a pornographic figure, albeit a refined one. In El Greco's *Laocoön,* done c. 1610, the stylized nudes of Mannerism have become figures of spiritual torment; his passionate religious fervor marked the death knell of that exuberant paganism, preciosity, and courtly escapism that inspired much of Mannerist art.

JOHN THE BAPTIST   VENUS & CUPID   MOSES   MINERVA   LAOCOÖN

"LADY AT HER TOILET"

How We Learned to Believe in Progress

The idea came chiefly from Condorcet,
whose own progress ended
when Robespierre had him arrested

Three centuries ago it might have taken Madame de Sévigné up to a month to move herself and her retinue from Paris to her home in the Dauphiné. Fifty years later the trip from Paris to Bordeaux by stagecoach still took a couple of weeks, and it was deemed something of a miracle when the most enlightened French statesman of the age, Anne Robert Jacques Turgot, reduced this to five and a half days by introducing lighter carriages (named *turgotines* in his honor) and putting an end to the repeated celebration of mass along the way.

When one considers that today the same distance can be covered by car in six hours, one sees what is meant by that "acceleration of history" that Turgot's friend Condorcet had the genius to foresee as an inherent feature of the march of progress. Tomorrow, if the more "progressive" among us have their way, the busiest bodies in the world will be transporting their managerial preoccupations across the oceans in even less time. Doubtless there are others, after them, who will take up the technological hue and cry, claiming that the welfare of some macroempire in petrochemicals or frozen foods

makes it imperative that instant transport be provided between Amsterdam and New Orleans or Chicago and Sydney. Yet one may wonder if somewhere along this course we may not shoot past the point of diminishing returns.

I write, admittedly, as a pessimist who has a good deal less faith in progress than had that exemplary futurist Condorcet. He it was who fired the imagination of Claude Henri de Saint-Simon, the founder of French socialism, who long before James Burnham conceived the idea of technocracy and the "managerial revolution," just as he inspired Auguste Comte, the father of sociology and the theorist, if not the founder, of the modern bureaucratic state. It was because he had been brought up on Condorcet that Alexis de Tocqueville could describe the "progressive development of equality" as an "irresistible revolution" destined to overcome all obstacles in its path. Others had preceded him in conceiving of a truly universal history, but Condorcet was the first to try to chart it in intellectual terms—that is, as a chronicle of man's long endeavor to triumph over ignorance, barbarism, and superstition. He anticipated Hegel, and thus Marx, with the result that faith in progress is now as triumphantly enthroned beyond the Iron Curtain as it is here with us.

It would, however, be misleading to

claim that Condorcet singlehandedly invented the notion of progress as something inherent in the historical development of the human race. This idea was, more properly speaking, the invention of an entire century—the eighteenth—and found expression in the writings of many of its foremost thinkers, from the skeptical Voltaire to the more sanguine Adam Smith. So fixed a feature of our mental horizon has it become that it is somewhat surprising to realize that this notion of progress, which has galvanized the millions, overthrown states, built and destroyed cities, transformed the landscape, and girdled the globe, boasts a very recent pedigree. As a social "fact of life," it is barely two centuries old. Neither the Greeks nor the Romans, who tended to hark back nostalgically to a Golden Age from which mankind had degenerated, ever envisaged anything remotely resembling our idea of progress, any more than did the European Middle Ages, obsessed as they were by the Augustinian notion of original sin, the prospect of a Second Coming, and the impending end of the world.

That it fell to Condorcet to chart not only the past but the future of human progress was something of an accident. Logically, that honor should have fallen to his friend and mentor Turgot, who in a lecture delivered at the Sorbonne in 1750 declared that "the total mass of the human species, through alternating periods of calm and agitation, good and evil, forever marches, albeit at a slow pace, towards a greater perfection." Turgot at the time was just twenty-three, and if he had gone on to write those *Discourses on Universal History* that he here briefly sketched, there is little doubt that they would now rank with Montesquieu's *Spirit of the Laws* as one of the epoch-making works of the century. But Turgot was a man of action as much as a thinker, and his duties as provincial administrator and later as a minister of Louis XVI made inordinate claims on his time. He was also, to judge by at least one of his letters to Condorcet, of a somewhat indolent disposition. Condorcet, on the other hand, was a workhorse whose writings came to fill sixteen volumes. They include a *Life of Turgot,* written after his friend's death, and, of course, the magnum opus that made him famous, the *Esquisse d'un tableau historique des progrès de l'esprit humain,* the *Sketch for a Historical Table of the Progress of the Human Mind.*

This work, curiously enough, was not undertaken until 1793, more than forty years after Turgot had first thrown out the idea that man's development, though subject to crises and calamities, moves in a generally upward direction. Like *Don Quixote,* Condorcet's *Esquisse* was the brain child of confinement, if not of actual incarceration. Not the least extraordinary thing about this almost rhapsodic credo in the inevitable betterment of the human species is that it was composed in the shadow of the guillotine and at a time when France seemed to have sunk back into an abyss of tyrannical violence and passion. So confident was its author that tomorrow is bound to be better that he could prophesy, "the moment will arrive when the sun will shine only on free men, who recognize no other master than their reason: when tyrants and slaves, priests and their stupid or hypocritical tools will exist only in history or on the stage."

Though the *Esquisse* is now read only by scholars, its influence over the first half of the nineteenth century was enormous, almost comparable to that which the *Communist Manifesto* continues to exercise to this day. It would be difficult to name a revolutionary—from Marx to Proudhon—who was not weaned on it. It provided a gospel for several generations of British utilitarians, thus contributing to the development of modern socialism as well as to liberalism. Probably more than any other single work it helped transform what had begun as an idea into a doctrine. In 1864 Pope Pius IX, seeing in it a dogma no less implacable than his own, had it placed on the Syllabus of Errors. It only remained for Dr. Emile Coué to popularize the cult of progress in his famous formula: "Every day in every way I am getting better and better."

It is, of course, unfair to judge a notion by the extremes to which its vulgarization can lead, but such juxtapositions can be illuminating. What begins as a dazzling promise can all too easily become a blight, exercising a blackmail spell as despotic as the oppression it was meant to banish. "Oh Liberty, what crimes are committed in thy name!" could just as easily be applied to the noble ideal of progress. Madame Roland, who uttered that desperate cry, was, as it happened, the friend of many of Condorcet's Girondist companions. Like her, he ended up the victim of the revolutionary momentum he did so much to foster.

Of his youth we know little beyond the fact that Marie Jean Antoine Nicolas de Caritat, to give him his full name, was born on September 17, 1743, in the little town of Ribemont, near Saint-Quentin in Picardy. His father, a cavalry captain, was killed in battle one month after the boy's birth, and he was brought up by his mother. That he should have achieved immortality as the Marquis de Condorcet would have been an anomaly in any other century but the eighteenth, when it seems to have been felt—in France, at any rate—that revolution could be warded off

by mass-producing patents of nobility. In the church registers that have survived, his father, Antoine de Caritat, is invariably listed as Chevalier. The Caritats were originally from Provence, and it was only through an accident of marriage that they came into possession of the Château de Condorcet, perched in the foothills of the Dauphiné some distance to the east of Grignan.

From her first husband as well as from her father, a fiscal official, Condorcet's mother had inherited a comfortable dowry. Haunted by the fear that the adversities that had removed her two husbands might likewise overtake her one and only son, she dedicated him to the Virgin, and, not content with that, dressed him in girls' clothing. This fact doubtless explains the inordinate and almost feminine sensitivity he displayed as an adult. The eighteenth century, with its powdered wigs and slippers, was as feminine an epoch as Europe has ever known, and in Condorcet's case the two forces—*Mutter* and *Zeitgeist*—were pulling in the same direction. One result of this was a detestation of cruelty, which led him to give up hunting and even to refrain from killing insects, unless—as he once explained in a letter to Turgot—"they are doing a lot of harm." The same abhorrence of suffering led him to condemn slavery, the feudal iniquities of the *ancien régime,* and the "barbarous" practices that European merchants and colonizers were introducing into Africa, Asia, and, incidentally, America.

Entrusted to the care of a Catholic tutor when he was nine, the young Condorcet was later sent to two Jesuit schools, in Reims and Paris. An excessively shy, introverted student, he soon revealed himself as a whiz in mathematics. At sixteen his oral defense of a complex problem of analysis so dazzled the panel of judges who examined him that D'Alembert, who was one of them, made himself his mentor and ultimately his friend. For the rest, Condorcet's eight years with the Jesuits seem to have left him with a bitter taste in his mouth. He read and learned to admire Pascal, but his gods were Descartes and Voltaire—the fathers of modern rationalism—and Rousseau, whose genius sparked the French Revolution.

His schooling over, his family sought to have him follow in his father's footsteps, but he wanted none of the army. In time, the eighteen-year-old "geometer" was allowed to return to Paris. For a while he stayed in a rented room, then went to live with a publisher named Suard and his wife, in a rather curious *ménage à trois* in which Condorcet has been described as playing the part of "platonic lover." To the amazement of those who came to know him well, he worked twelve hours a day, unheard of in this easygoing silk-stocking age.

The first product of this industrious cerebration, delivered when he was barely twenty-two, was an essay on internal calculus that won the praise of D'Alembert, who presented it to the French Academy of Sciences. Joseph Louis Lagrange, whom E. T. Bell has called "the greatest and most modest mathematician of the eighteenth century," was equally impressed, and the patronage of these two savants was enough to get Condorcet admitted to the academy when he was only twenty-six. His mathematical endeavors, chiefly aimed at achieving a synthesis between differential and integral calculus, continued to occupy his mind right up to the year of his death, though from 1770 on it was more a pastime than it was anything else.

It was D'Alembert, the scientific editor of the great *Encyclopédie,* who channeled the young man's energies in a more practical, less theoretical direction. In the salon of Julie de Lespinasse, the "Muse of the Encyclopedists," he was introduced to the leading intellectual lights—from the philosopher Helvétius to Marmontel, Franklin, the Abbé Morellet, the Duc de la Rochefoucauld and his mother, the Comtesse de Boufflers, Condillac, Turgot, Quesnay, and that sagacious Scotsman, Adam Smith, who came to France in the 1760's to learn the gospel of free trade. It was with D'Alembert that Condorcet made the pilgrimage to Geneva in 1770 to meet Voltaire. The old man kept them at Ferney for two whole weeks, and went on to write more than sixty letters to Condorcet, whom he hailed as "greater than Fontenelle" and as destined, with D'Alembert, to "form a new France."

It was likewise D'Alembert who had Condorcet named Perpetual Secretary of the Academy of Sciences in 1773. Years of contact with his protégé had enabled him to penetrate the somewhat cold, laconic air he wore in public. To Julie de Lespinasse and her witty friends this tall, diffident young man who often blushed when spoken to, stumbled over his words, and even bit his fingernails to hide his embarrassment, must at first have seemed hopelessly gauche. But with the years he gained assurance, and people came to realize that his preoccupied air concealed a penetrating judgment. Slightly stoop-shouldered, with a large head and torso that contrasted oddly with his spindly legs, he bore a faint resemblance to a Max Beerbohm cartoon; but the head was anything but empty, just as the tongue was not necessarily idle. If he was often silent at these *après-dîners philosophiques,* it was from a reluctance to say anything nasty, for "*le bon Condorcet*" strove to exemplify in his behavior what he had come, through Rousseau's influence, to believe—that man is fundamentally good.

Julie de Lespinasse was so impressed that in the idyllic "portrait" she later drew of him she wrote that "his mind has the grace and facility of Voltaire's, the *piquant* of Fontenelle's, the bite of Pascal's, the depth and perspicacity of Newton's . . . and if you think I am exaggerating in what I say, judge M. Condorcet for yourself, talk with him, read what he has written; speak to him about philosophy, belles lettres, the sciences, the arts, government, jurisprudence, and when you have heard him out, you will find yourself saying a hundred times over that this is the most astounding man you have ever heard. There is nothing he is ignorant of, not even the things that are furthest removed from his own tastes and occupations: he will tell you the latest sayings of the Palace and the genealogy of the people at the Court, details about the police, the names of the bonnets that are in fashion. In short, nothing is beneath his attention, and his memory is so prodigious that he has never forgotten anything."

Mlle de Lespinasse, in her gushing generosity, was here yielding to that springtime rapture of the soul that Rousseau had made romantically fashionable with his *Nouvelle Héloïse.* More to the point was D'Alembert's crisp definition of Condorcet as "a snow-covered volcano." As Secretary of the Academy of Sciences, he lived up to the appellation by turning his post into a kind of intellectual fortress, from which he periodically sniped away at priests, obscurantists, and all those in league with "the powers of darkness." Most of these "sorties" took the form of *Eloges,* which were written to honor former members of the Academy of Sciences or other memorable Frenchmen. Occasionally, however, Condorcet delivered himself of an anonymous broadside—as in the *Lettre d'un théologien* (1774) in which, after ironically praising priests for all the wars, massacres, burnings at the stake, et cetera, they had caused, he boldly announced that the time would soon come when theology would no longer be regarded as of sufficient interest to warrant ridicule.

That same year the new millennium seemed to have dawned when the playboy king, Louis XV, died and was succeeded by his far more serious grandson. Louis XVI's first act was to name Turgot minister of the navy, and then minister of finance. Aware of the difficulty Condorcet had been having trying to make do on the meager stipend provided by his mother, Turgot had his friend appointed director of the national mint. For the next fifteen years Condorcet thus lived on the public payroll, inhabiting an apartment in the recently completed Hôtel des Monnaies.

The new millennium, as it happened, lasted a brief two years. As minister of finance, Turgot set out to introduce reforms that might have saved the monarchy from its fate. Condorcet, who was one of his three principal advisers, saw him almost every day, urging him to move faster, regardless of the hidebound opposition he faced from most of the clergy and nobility. The range of his brain-trusting interests may be gauged by the fact that he urged the creation of a botanical garden at Hyères, on the Mediterranean, for the cultivation of tropical plants; worked on a project to build ice-breaking barges, to ease the harassing problem of feeding Paris through the freezing winter months; prepared a plan for improving the French canal system; and tried (with his fellow scientist Lavoisier) to develop a machine for desalting water.

Though nominally in charge of the monarchy's coinage, Condorcet was in fact Turgot's unofficial minister of propaganda. His pamphlet *Réflexions sur le commerce des blés,* advocating a wholesale abolition of administrative controls on the sale and transport of food products, anticipated the arguments Adam Smith was to develop into an entire philosophy of economics in *The Wealth of Nations.* A second pamphlet, advocating the abolition of the medieval work quotas (*corvées*) that many French peasants were still forced to provide their landlords, stirred up so much opposition that in January, 1776, Versailles ordered it seized and burned. Turgot fell just four months later, victim of a court cabal. In a letter written to Voltaire to apprise him of the end of "a beautiful dream," Condorcet said that he was going to return to geometry and philosophy, adding that the thought of working for his sole glory left him cold "when one has flattered oneself for a while that one was working for the public good."

He spent the next decade composing more *Eloges* and writing the biographies of Voltaire and Turgot, which remained for a generation thereafter the standard texts on these two men. Named by D'Alembert as the executor of his will, he vainly sought to save the letters Frederick the Great had written him. (They, too, were burned.) He also pursued his mathematical investigations, now interestingly directed toward the development of probability analysis, with an idea to applying it to population statistics and insurance policies. Though forced to admit, with Hume, that human events cannot be predicted through any purely deductive and a priori system of analysis, he nevertheless expressed the belief that even the darkest and most complex of human motivations could systematically be scrutinized, brought to light, and even "measured with some exactitude." "The more we know about a motive, the less irresistible is its force" was, roughly speaking, his formulation of a principle that might be called, without exaggeration, the first principle of psychology. That Condorcet should thus unwittingly have anticipated Freud is not as surprising as it might at first sight seem; for here as elsewhere he was only following in the footsteps of Descartes, the man who had proclaimed self-analysis and introspection to be the touchstone of cognition.

In 1786 Condorcet married Sophie de Grouchy, whose passion for Voltaire and Rousseau delighted Condorcet as much as it had outraged her mother—who had had their infamous volumes committed to the flames. Kindhearted, distinguished, and good-looking, she was a young and sprightly twenty-two to the Marquis's sedate forty-three—a disparity in age that soon set tongues wagging about the scandalous liaisons her marriage to Condorcet was supposed to have covered up. There is no reason to believe a word of this malicious gossip, for if it was a shotgun wedding, the alarm was premature. Sophie de Condorcet's child was born in April of 1790, nine months after the fall of the Bastille. This accident of chronology later inspired the historian Michelet to pen a more than usually dithyrambic passage (in *Les Femmes de la révolution*) in which he declared that it was only now, in the lurid afterglow of that epic demolition, that she fully realized the deep reserves of passion that were stored up in this "seemingly cold man," coming to love "this great citizen, this tender and deep soul who cherished, as though they were his own, the hope and happiness of the human race."

That Condorcet, like many another French nobleman, welcomed the revolution is, of course, undeniable. He was an enthusiastic promoter of the metric system, which he helped to develop. He shed no tears over the mass scrapping of titles (including his own) that followed the extraordinary "Oath of the Tennis Court" of June, 1789; and though he felt that there might be some utility in adopting the "Esquire" that Jefferson and others had favored in a now liberated America, he was adamantly opposed to the maintenance of baptism "because theology is worth no more than feudalism." He helped draft the Declaration of the Rights of Man and opposed the institution of a bicameral legislature, claiming to have proved *arithmetically* the absurdity of any such institution. He deplored the king's attempt to flee from France, was named one of the secretaries of the Legislative Assembly of 1791 after being elected to it by the citizens of Paris, and was the principal drafter of a five-stage project for universal education that was taken over by the Directory and Napoleon with only minor modifications.

Again elected to the Convention in September, 1792, this time as the representative of five different departments, he voted for the establishment of the Republic, and though he felt that it was not the Convention's job to try the king for conspiring with the enemies of France, he voted for his condemnation, but not his execution—which he felt was too "inhumane." He was even more upset when, after four months of labor, his project for a new constitution was rejected by an increasingly turbulent assembly. The fragments of his writings that have survived from these years chart his dismay over the increasingly lawless and bloody march of events—like the mass burning of genealogical records that was celebrated on the Place Vendôme (renamed Place des Piques) in February, 1793. His misgivings were voiced in a publication called *Journal d'instruction sociale,* in which he attacked "the political charlatans . . . of a mediocre talent . . . who think they are Caesars and Cromwells."

The last straw was the adoption, virtually without debate, of a hastily drafted constitution that had been summarily examined by the Committee of Public Safety in just one day. Compared to the months of careful work that had gone into the elaboration of the American Constitution, this was all too obviously an instrument hurriedly fashioned to perpetuate the tyranny of a fanatical oligarchy. Condorcet would have been better advised to hold his peace—but no, the normally snow-covered crater now blew its top. The result was another anonymous pamphlet, this time accusing the new constitution of secreting the "germs of royalty" and of being designed to favor "the audacity of some scoundrel who might wish to mount the throne."

The fat was in the fire. It was no secret to anyone that the author of this pamphlet was Condorcet, and that the "scoundrel" it was aimed at was Robespierre. A fellow Jacobin named Chabot now rose to denounce "this man who because he has sat among the learned in the Academy imagines that he has the right to give laws to the French Republic." The Convention agreed, voting that Condorcet be arrested and his papers impounded, because "there will be found the thread of the conspiracy."

The Committee of Public Safety lost no time in carrying out this resolution. Several police commissioners were sent to apprehend him at his secretary's lodgings on the Left Bank. Unable to find him there, they moved on to the suburban village of Auteuil, where Condorcet and his wife shared an apart-

ment in a modest house. Here they found Madame, or rather *la citoyenne* Condorcet, calmly seated upstairs alone. Her brother-in-law, a doctor named Cabanis, had arranged to have Condorcet escorted back into Paris by two friends. As medical students they had once lived on the rue Servandoni, near the Church of Saint-Sulpice, with a Madame Vernet, who took in lodgers, and it was here that they had found a place for Condorcet to hide.

It was here, in a small upstairs room overlooking a tree-shaded inner court, that Condorcet spent the last eight months of his life, composing that extraordinary paean to progress, that credo in the infinite perfectibility of the human species, the *Esquisse d'un tableau historique des progrès de l'esprit humain.* He spent each morning in bed, writing on a tablet, his feet enveloped in blankets. He would come down to have lunch in Madame Vernet's ground-floor dining room, and the *après-dîner* that followed in the salon, often till seven or eight in the evening, would enable him to discuss the events of the day with regular visitors. They included Cabanis, Antoine Dyannyère, his secretary Cardot, a mathematician called Sarret, who had secretly married Madame Vernet, and most astonishing of all, the Jacobin deputy Marcoz, who, though also a lodger, loyally promised his landlady that he would keep the secret.

During the early months of this "captivity" his wife Sophie visited him two or three times a week, disguised as a peasant. Realizing that she might be followed, she made a habit of mingling with the crowds that swarmed down to the Place de la Révolution every day to watch the guillotine in action. To support herself, a three-year-old daughter, an aged governess, and an ailing sister, she opened a lingerie shop on the rue Saint-Honoré and painted cameos and miniature portraits of persons who, like her husband, had been outlawed or condemned and wished to bequeath their likenesses to friends and relatives.

It was also Sophie who persuaded Condorcet to stop working on the "jus-

tification," or apologia (of his role during the revolution), to which he had devoted his first weeks at Madame Vernet's. At the end of October, 1793, a number of his Girondist friends were beheaded, and he now realized that all hope of forgiveness was vain so long as Robespierre remained in power. The next four months were consequently devoted to the writing of his *Esquisse,* a work he had been planning for some time. Most of his papers had been impounded, but the friends who came to see him were able to supply him with an occasional book or reference; it is nonetheless true that most of the *Esquisse* was drawn from the reserves of his prodigious memory.

He still found time to work on mathematical problems, as well as on a pet project aimed at developing an error-free language similar to those of geometry and mathematics—an interesting anticipation of what certain logical positivists have recently been trying to do. He also penned a memorandum designed to teach people a simple, sure-fire method of counting, dispatching it sheet by sheet to his wife in Auteuil.

Early in 1794 Sophie was forced to ask for a divorce—to save herself and her daughter from the vengeful reprisals of the Jacobins. Six months having expired since the issuance of the warrant for Condorcet's arrest, he was now considered a traitor who had joined France's enemies in exile. Condorcet, for his part, was increasingly tortured by the thought that he was exposing his "second mother," as he called Madame Vernet, to the death penalty by letting her shelter an "exile." Toward the end of March a stranger warned Madame Vernet that people would be visiting the house the next day "in search of salt-petre"—then needed for gunpowder—and advised her to hide anything precious she might happen to have. Condorcet, who overheard this speech, decided the time had come to leave. Disguised in a Phrygian wool bonnet and the revolutionary *carmagnole* (a short waistcoat-jacket), he slipped out of Madame Vernet's house at ten o'clock the next morning—March 25, 1794. His fellow mathematician Sarret accompanied him up the street past the grim Luxembourg prison, from which every morning tumbrils full of victims were transported to the guillotine. They managed to skirt a barrier on the rue de Vaugirard, and once beyond the city limits on the Plaine de Montrouge, Condorcet bid Sarret farewell, saying that he was going to seek asylum with a friend who lived in the village of Fontenay-aux-Roses, some distance to the south and west.

The friend was Suard, with whom Condorcet had once lodged in the impecunious sixties and whom he had later installed, along with his wife, at the Hôtel des Monnaies. But when he got to their house at Fontenay-aux-Roses, he learned that the Suards were in Paris. Condorcet went to hide in a nearby quarry; he spent the night there and came back the next day, only to be told that the couple were still away. He had to spend a second night out of doors. The next morning he found Suard and his wife at home. But their news was not encouraging: the feeling in the village was "detestable" and they could not even trust their own maid. Suard told him he would go back to Paris and try to get him a passport, and it was agreed that the suspect maid would somehow be lured away from the house, so that Condorcet could spend the night there.

Suard must have been dismayed to see this haggard-looking apparition, for Condorcet had now spent two nights in the quarry, and though he carried a razor in his pocket, he had probably acquired a tramplike growth of beard. To make matters worse, a rolling stone had opened a gash in his leg. Suard and his wife bandaged it up, but then, fearful of arousing the maid's suspicions, they sent him on his way with an almost empty stomach.

Hunger must now have gotten the better of his caution. At one o'clock that afternoon Condorcet entered an inn in the nearby village of Clamart. Unwittingly he was sticking his head into the lion's mouth: the innkeeper, one Louis Crespinet, was head of the local militia, and there were with him at this moment two of the "most furious terrorists" in the neighborhood. The legend subsequently was put out that Condorcet aroused their suspicion by ordering an omelette, and that when the innkeeper asked: "How many eggs?" he replied, "A dozen"—an answer no good plebeian could ever have made.

Asked for his papers, Condorcet was unable to produce them. The local *Comité de surveillance* was alerted and the suspect taken to a nearby church, now a place for the dispensation of revolutionary justice. In vain did Condorcet try to persuade them that he was Pierre Simon, a humble valet who had worked for several honorable Frenchmen—whom he named. His inquisitors could not understand why he had no papers, nor why he could not remember the name of the inn where he claimed to have spent the night. He was searched: in addition to a watch, a penknife, a pencil, and a razor, a small volume of Horace's poems was extracted from his pockets, and this was enough to condemn him.

No longer able to walk, Condorcet was heaved into a requisitioned cart and transported to a makeshift prison in Bourg-la-Reine, now Bourg-Egalité. Here he spent the remainder of that somber Thursday and all of Friday. At four o'clock on the afternoon of Saturday, March 29, the jailer entered his room and found the prisoner stretched face-downward on the ground. The medical officer summoned a few hours later declared that he had died of *"apopléxie sanguine"*—or as we would say, of a stroke.

This tragic denouement seemed intolerably pathetic to Condorcet's admirers, who put it out that he had taken poison, which he had kept hidden in a ring. How the revolutionaries who arrested him could have overlooked such a giveaway embellishment no one took the trouble to explain. The first engrav-

ings of this tragic end, which date from 1795, portray the martyr with a glass of water as well as the lethal ring: he has slumped over from his chair, and his carefully undraped torso is stretched out on the bed. The jailer, who has just opened the door, gapes at the dismal scene with imperishable stupefaction.

After Robespierre's overthrow, his fellow deputy Daunou suggested that the Convention honor the memory of the prophet who, notwithstanding "the disastrous conditions under which he wrote . . . speaks about the Revolution with nothing but enthusiasm." With the willing co-operation of his widow, 3,600 posthumous copies of the *Esquisse* were accordingly printed up and sold in 1795, barely eighteen months after his death.

Today, one can only marvel at the assurance with which, in the midst of these revolutionary upheavals, Condorcet could trace the ten epochs into which he divided human history—from the earliest tribal forms, made up of warriors and hunters, down to the eighth epoch, marked by the invention of the printing press, and the ninth, ushered in by the proclamation of Descartes's scientific method and crowned by "that new doctrine . . . of the indefinite perfectibility of the human race of which Turgot, Price, and Priestley have been the first and most illustrious apostles."

The tenth and final epoch, opened by the heroic thunder of the revolution, was, Condorcet declared, to be marked by "the future progress of the human mind." In its opening paragraphs he bluntly states, "Our hopes as to the future of the human species can be reduced to these three important points: the destruction of the inequality between nations; the progress of equality within the same people; and finally, the perfecting of man."

It is astonishing how many of the developments Condorcet declared to be inevitable have, in fact, occurred. The European colonialism he so passionately denounced has withered away, much as he predicted. Though complete social equality is still only an ideal, it is one to which most countries and politicians now pay assiduous lip service. Fortunes may not "naturally tend towards equality," as Condorcet claimed, but excessive disparities of wealth are now generally regarded as scandalous, and the idea that social security should palliate for obvious inequalities has become, since Keynes, one of the cornerstones of modern economics.

Condorcet was equally emphatic in proclaiming the eventual equality of the sexes. He looked forward, too, to the "inevitable" development of the calculating machines that Pascal and Leibnitz had invented, which he predicted would one day be applied to the solution of political as well as other problems—something we have seen come to pass within the last thirty years. Struck by the facility with which a young mathematics student could pick up what it had taken Newton years of concentrated effort to develop, he also foresaw that "acceleration of history" that has become the most formidable, and in some ways the most frightening, phenomenon of our times.

What Condorcet did not foresee, of course, was almost as important as what he did. In yoking together Liberty, Equality, and Progress, he assumed that this heroic troika was bound to gallop forward in a smoothly parallel course. Nothing could be less certain. A superabundance of liberty can lead to chaos and to liberty's pendular opposite, tyranny; the pursuit of equality can lead to a curtailment of individual liberty; and the pursuit of progress, as the ecologists now warn us, is being purchased at the cost of human *Lebensraum,* of a freedom to be something better than a cramped, congested, pollution-dogged, and increasingly regimented robot.

At one point in his *Esquisse* Condorcet was troubled by the thought that the steady increase in numbers of the human species might eventually block the further amelioration of its lot. But he hastened to banish the specter, re-

marking that such a nightmarish prospect was still "very far removed from us," and adding that "nothing frightening would result from it, either for the happiness of the human species or its indefinite perfectibility, if one supposed that with time the progress of reason has marched in tempo with those of the sciences and arts." This was a gigantic if: in fact, history has since accelerated and the human race proliferated far faster than even he envisaged. Contemporary man seems only slightly more reasonable than he was in the days of the good Marquis, and his perfectibility seems more tentative and finite than ever.

This, however, is almost certainly the moral to be drawn from his work and his example. Not for nothing was Condorcet, like Descartes, a mathematician. Nor was it an accident that he lived in the eighteenth century, the century that saw the Newtonian system enthroned in the philosophical firmament thanks to the graceful periods of François Marie Arouet, better known to the world as Monsieur de Voltaire. The idea of progress as an inevitable, unlimited, never-ending movement was like the fire that Prometheus brought to earth, an idea stolen from the starry heavens.

Now this conception of the cosmos —as something infinitely grandiose, sublime, and knowable—is dead. It was killed when Michelson and Morley determined that light has a finite speed; and until and unless it is discovered that there are rays that travel faster than light, most of the universe is destined to remain for us a *camera obscura.*

Eighty years ago Jules Verne could imagine top-hatted future travelers cruising comfortably to the moon aboard a luxurious craft lifted into space by propellers. Today we know just what it costs to lift spacemen from the surface of the moon; we also know what neither Verne nor Condorcet suspected—that the surface of Venus is too incandescent to permit enjoyable weekend visits to that planet. Within the next decade or two, we may be able to land a team of astronauts on the

frozen wastes of Mars, but the cost of more ambitious explorations of our solar system, to say nothing of our galaxy, seems too prohibitive even to be contemplated.

Thus each advance of knowledge has the paradoxical effect not of widening but of narrowing the future range of investigation. Not only has the steady expansion of knowledge failed to make men better human beings, as Condorcet so confidently assumed; like industrial growth, science itself breeds its own environmental pollution. Not long ago, Professor Kenneth Boulding of the University of Colorado's Institute of Behavioral Science warned that "all growth processes eventually run into diminishing rates of growth . . . It is quite easy to visualize a situation, perhaps even in a hundred years, in which the stock of knowledge will be so large that the whole effort of the knowledge industry will have to be devoted to transmitting it from one generation to the next. Education is an insatiable monster that will eventually gobble up all of research and at that moment the growth of science will come to an end."

I write, as I say, as a pessimist: as someone who feels that while the infinite is a concept suited to eschatology or mathematics, it is one that cannot long be applied to the mundane realities of everyday life. This is a bitter truth, for it goes against the grain of what, partly thanks to Monsieur Condorcet, we have most of us been brought up to believe. We are now discovering that man can suffer from an overdose of Progress no less than from a surfeit of Liberty. Progress for the sake of progress is ultimately as pointless as any movement that, having lost its bearings, seeks only to perpetuate its own momentum. When growth turns into growthmanship, as Vance Packard has demonstrated, the result is not health; it is more like a cancer.

Curtis Cate's progress in French letters, marked in 1970 by his book on the flier-poet Saint-Exupéry, will soon be marked anew by a a biography of George Sand.

GILGAMESH

This Sumerian epic is about Gilgamesh and
Enkidu—and friendship and life and death.
It is the very beginning of literature, and
the story of its survival is itself a miracle

By NIGEL DENNIS

Our forefathers spoke happily of "The
Dawn of History" and "The Dawn of
Civilization"—and very nice it must
have been to be standing at high noon
oneself, watching the epochs of the past
turning up like reversed clockwork
until they faded out of sight in the
darkness of the small hours. It was all so
tidy, seen that way, and it not only
made history teachable and consequen-
tial but gave an admirable stability to
present existence.

In the matter of civilization, only two
dawns were recognized as such—the
light descending on the Holy Land, and
sunrise over the Athenian Acropolis.
These two, uniting happily over central
Italy, gradually illuminated all Europe
and threw a special luster on wigs, frock
coats, and quill pens. Only the antiquary
meddled with other dawns, known to
have made brief, eccentric appearances
over China and Egypt; these were
clearly never intended by the Great
Clockmaker to progress beyond some
vague, exotic breakfast hour.

From this comfortable regularity, we
have gone into a timetable that promises nothing but an infinite regression.
The dawn not only refuses to dawn with
its old punctuality, it takes place earlier

and earlier and has already displaced all
the hours back to midnight. It shows no
sign of stopping before the previous
day, which makes a mess of our imagination, our books, our sense of historical position. No sooner do we accustom
ourselves to a new dawn than another
appears behind it, and we are without
any way of knowing how long this ret-
rograde procedure is likely to go on.

To take but one example, when
James Mellaart stopped excavating the
Turkish site of Çatal Hüyük, he had
reached the twelfth city and was sure
that there were still earlier ones lying in
wait below. And all the cities he had un-
buried were worthy of being the dawn
of civilization, showing every evidence
of complex administration, metalwork,
handicrafts, luxury goods. But about
8000 B.C. he was obliged to stop, already
thousands of years earlier than the famous command: "Let there be light."

What we think of as civilization is
always the way we live now—or was
until this century made us wonder if we
were civilized at all. The inhabitants of
Çatal Hüyük lived in one immense
blockhouse of a city: when they went
home, they climbed a ladder on the
outer wall, walked over the communal

roofs until they reached their particular
flats, and then went down into the
bosoms of their families by way of the
chimney. We do not feel at home with
such behavior; practical though it may
have been, it gives the impression of a
strange and distant people whose ways
were generally quite different from our
own. The only dawns we feel really
happy with are those with which we can
connect ourselves and from which the
passage of the sun to our own day seems
marked and recognizable.

At the present moment we have only
one such dawn, and a late one at that,
little older than 4000 B.C. This is the civilization of Sumer, the world of cities that
lay above the Persian Gulf between the
Tigris and the Euphrates and was not
known even to have existed until a little
more than a century ago. It is a good example of the regressive dawn. By 1860
the dawn of Genesis was known to have
behind it the dawn of Assyria, and behind Assyria, the dawn of old Babylon.
An archaeological dig sent out by the
British Museum to exhume Assyrian
Nineveh found Sumer rising behind it
instead. The awakening was particularly startling for British Biblical
scholars because it included, inscribed

Gilgamesh stands triumphant, with two human-headed bulls he has overcome, in this inlay panel from the sound box of a harp found in a royal tomb at Ur.

on clay tablets, a flood story much like that of Noah and the Ark, which was supposed to be sacrosanct to the Book of Genesis and thus had no right to appear over the horizon a millennium or more before.

It is these clay tablets, and the tales they tell, that link us closely to "the black-headed people" (as the Sumerians called themselves) and allow us to trace our descent from them in a way we cannot do with the ladder men of Çatal Hüyük. In the first place, the tablets mark the dawn of the written word —at least, as of today: other, earlier dawns of writing may still be awaiting discovery. There are a few words in Hebrew and Arabic that stem from the Sumerian; in Malta today, the inhabitants still use some common words that were current in Sumer six thousand years ago. Moreover, thanks to the discovery of thousands and thousands of these little clay tablets in the past hundred years, we can trace the evolution of the letter itself. The earliest examples of Sumerian letters are simply charming little pictures: "He goes to eat" is expressed merely by a boot in a forward position, followed by a face with a bowl to its lips. A slave woman is

simply a pudendum and what appears to be three meat pies; in fact, they are stylized representations of the hills from which the female slaves of Sumer came. But as the centuries passed and writing became a highly professional craft, the tablets showed these little pictures losing their direct and primitive charm and changing into stylized symbols, leaving only vestigial traces of their picturesque beginnings. Inherited by the Sumerians' successors—the Semitic Akkadians, the Babylonians, the Assyrians—they at last became purely literary markings, no longer identifiable by their earlier forms and understood only by scribes and students.

This process is often reversed in the matter of what the tablets have to say. It was the beginners, the Sumerians, who had the genius of storytelling and even of sophisticated aphorisms. Much of what they recorded has been lost, but fortunately, the Semitic Akkadians set their own scribes to translating the Sumerian language and copying Sumerian records. Thus it is that the pieces of one fragmented Sumerian poem or story may crop up anywhere in the Middle East, in various languages of

various periods, and it is such pieces, brought together by scholars in the field, that must be patiently reassembled into something like the original.

Perhaps such patchwork is never quite the "original." We are told that in ancient Greece there was a sect of devout people who worshiped Homer as a god and paid tribute to him by writing . . . Homer. Something of the same kind may have happened to the works of the Sumerians. A basic product of the past, they were widely edited, plagiarized, expanded, and corrupted. What reaches us today is a wonderful book of literature punctuated with endless question marks as to authorship and full of missing or corrupt pages.

What remains shows us that these workers in the dawn survived long enough to develop into a highly sophisticated people who stood, in their own eyes, at the very meridian of civilization. When we read one of their laconic little poems,

My wife is thanking God for all he has
   given her;
My mother is prostrate beside the
   sacred river;
There is not, methinks, much hope
   of dinner.

From Clay Tablet to Printed Page

A few episodes of the Gilgamesh cycle had appeared in Sumerian by the middle of the third millennium B.C., but by the eighteenth century B.C., the epic had been enlarged and unified in its Akkadian version, on tablets like the one at near right. Next to the tablet is an enlargement of the outlined passage. On the opposite page are, left to right, a line copy of the passage, a syllabic transliteration in the Akkadian language, and a translation of these sixteen lines provided by Dr. David I. Owen, who also supplied the photographs and drawings on these two pages.

ALL: UNIVERSITY MUSEUM, UNIVERSITY OF PENNSYLVANIA. PHOTOGRAPHS AND DRAWINGS PUBLISHED WITH THE PERMISSION OF PROF. AKE W. SJÖBERG, CURATOR OF TABLET COLLECTION

we know that the dawn is already far behind, because urbanity and pithiness, particularly at the expense of religion, come late in a people's development. First must come the legends, the sagas, the tales of Creation, the histories of the gods and heroes; hundreds of years are likely to elapse before the poet makes use of his inheritance with a tolerant smile. Moreover, even the earliest works of literature are apt to rest on a still more distant past, a past unchronicled at the time and more or less totally foreign to the sophisticates of a later millennium.

One of the earliest Sumerian works of literature, and by far the greatest, turns on their belief that neither a resurrection nor a last judgment awaited human beings after death. When a man "went into the mountain," which was the Sumerians' euphemism for dying, he became a shade, existing forever in a nebulous region under the earth, in almost total darkness, and feeding upon dust and clay. No salvation awaited him, however high or sacred his rank, because the gods had excepted only one man and woman from their decree of universal finality in death. These two were Ziusudra, a Noah-like figure known as the "Faraway One," and his wife: eternal life in a divine garden was the reward of the saviors of the human and animal kingdoms.

The Epic of Gilgamesh, which is the work referred to, is, among many other things, the first great lament for man's inconsolable death. Earliest of all epics, it is today the freshest and the closest to us, challenged in this respect only by the *Odyssey*. It is a chronicle of man's life identical in essence with what any man's life might be—a manhood of success and triumph, full of glamour and laughter, broken at its very height by the sudden blow of death and ending with a despairing, fruitless journey in search of rejuvenation and immortality. Today, when our own belief in a world to come has faded almost to nothing, carrying us back in our hopelessness to the Sumerians of five thousand years ago, the story that is told by this epic goes straight to the heart, and we share to the utmost the poignancy

c. 2800 B.C.	c. 2100 B.C.	c. 1750 B.C.	c. 1000 B.C.	
				dingir = god
				gemé = slave girl
				sag = head
				gud = ox
				šẽ = barley

This table shows how Sumerian writing evolved from pictographs to cuneiform symbols. The Sumerians died out around 2000 B.C., but their language was studied till the first century B.C.

of its beautiful, fatalistic conclusion:

> The moon waxes and wanes,
> The fish swims to the hook,
> The deer discovers the noose;
> At the bend, the chariot
> Turns and disappears;
> One day, the shepherd
> Goes into the mountain.
> One day, the king
> Takes to his bed,
> Empty sandals
> Attest his feet.*

Poetically, dramatically, even naturally, so despondent a conclusion demands an exhilarating beginning: there must be a brilliant dawn to justify such a clouded sunset. And *The Epic of Gilgamesh* supplies this necessity to the full. For half its length it is robust, roisterous, and bursting with enthusiasm; the confidence of its principal characters is so rude and deep that the gods themselves become uneasy. At last, they play their trump card, which is Death itself, and which is warranted only by the excessive vitality of the heroes.

The heroes are two in number. The first is Gilgamesh, king of Uruk, a city-state that is under the patronage of Inanna, goddess of love and war. Like King Arthur, Gilgamesh is a mighty creature of legend who might well have been a living king of the past. The Sumerian chroniclers have placed him fifth in

*The author has based his renderings of the poetry on the prose version of *The Epic of Gilgamesh* by Mrs. N. K. Saunders (Penguin).

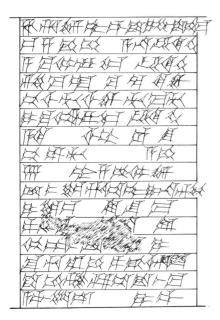

ḫa-ri-im-tum pi-ša i-pu-ša-am-ma
iz-za-kar-am a-na ᵈen-ki-du₁₀
a-ku-ul ak-lam ᵈen-ki-du₁₀
sí-ma-at ba-la-ṭi-im
šikaram ši-ti ši-im-ti ma-ti
i-ku-ul a-ak-lam ᵈen-ki-du₁₀
a-di ši-bé-e-šu
šikaram iš-ti-a-am
7 as-sà-am-mi-im
it-tap-šar kab-ta-tum i-na-an-gu
i-li-iṣ libba-šu-ma
pa-n[u-š]u i[t]-tam-ru
ul-tap-pi-it gallabum
šu-ḫu-ra-am pa-ga-ar-šu
ša-am-nam ip-ta-ša-aš-ma
a-wi-li-iš i-we

And the prostitute began to speak,
Saying to Enkidu,
"Eat bread, Enkidu,
[it is] the symbol of civilized life;
Drink beer, [it is] the custom of the land."
Enkidu ate bread
Until he was full;
He drank beer,
Seven goblets.
His mind reeled, he became giddy,
His heart *pounded,*
His face became *flushed.*
The barber *dressed*
The hair of his body.
He anointed himself with oil
And became a human being.

the line of kings that followed the Flood, before which all the cities of Sumer had been ruled by divinities. But the essence of Gilgamesh's tragedy is the fact that he himself is not wholly divine. Son of a local "goddess"—perhaps a temple priestess—and a king named "Fool" or "Demon," he was endowed by the Great Gods with perfect courage and perfect beauty—but not with immortality. No matter how big his triumphs, death must put an end to them: divine in life, he is mortal in death. He is thus the first true "hero" known to literature—first in the heroic line of vulnerable demigods such as Prometheus, Atlas, the Titans, Achilles. In Greek eyes, ordinary human beings were incapable of tragedy and best left to the comedy of such as Aristophanes; the gods, too, were unfit for tragedy because their immortality was assured. In between these extremes and partaking of both, stood the heroic demigod, tragic because his mortal fall was from divine heights. Christendom respects this pattern in the two persons of Jesus Christ, without which the Crucifixion would lose the splendor of its tragedy.

But the tragedy of his own mortality is not even suspected by the young Gilgamesh. Like any dashing young man of any period, he has no time to think about death; his days are spent in leading the young men astray and going after the women. The good citizens of Uruk are soon dismayed by such behavior and ask plaintively:

"Is this our king, is this our shepherd?
Where is the wisdom, where the charity?
Where two parts God, where One humanity?"

The Great Gods agree with the good citizens. They set the goddess of Creation to work and she, moistening her hands and molding clay, creates and throws onto the earth a brand-new man named Enkidu. He is as strong and as tough as Gilgamesh, and his function is to provide the erring king with a bosom friend of his own stature. Together, they will march out of Uruk and perform stupendous deeds—to the relief of the married men and the city fathers.

Enkidu is a wonderful character, but the tale of his creation and early life is a mythical imagining of the greatest interest. He falls into the world wild, shaggy, and totally innocent; he runs with the deer and lives an animal's life; he knows nothing of human society. But he has human hands and wits, and the local trapper soon finds to his despair that his snares and pitfalls are being neatly put out of action by the hand of a monstrous wild creature who runs on two legs. The trapper goes for advice to his old father, one of the minor characters in the epic who appear only for a moment and speak only a few lines and yet leave on the reader a deep impression of personal significance and vision. In this case, we are taken aback by the advice the old gentleman trots out without hesitation—that his son go

straight to Uruk, find a temple prostitute, and bring her to deal with Enkidu. This is done immediately and results in some of the most moving and extraordinary scenes of the epic: Enkidu's seduction; the terror of the animals when his smell becomes that of a human being; his despair at finding himself bereft of his natural innocence; his initiation by the prostitute into civilized habits such as drinking beer and milk from a bowl and combing his long hair. This remarkable sequence includes a touching stroke of art when the prostitute rips her own robe into two pieces and gives one of them to Enkidu, so that he may enter human society with a covering for his nakedness.

If one dwells on this succession of events, it is because this whole section of the epic reads like a string of echoes, each slightly off key to our ears but still seeming to identify itself with a familiar sound. Natural man has lost his innocence in a sort of primeval garden that is not quite Eden; the apple of the tree of knowledge is the body of a prostitute; a Delilah has found a shaggy Samson; an Adam has discovered his nakedness. None of it quite fits what we know, and yet we seem to know it, and to know it more deeply in our bones than we can ever know the *Iliad* or even subsequent sections of the epic itself. Tales of heroic glory, the hammering out and shaping of weapons, the grand marches against the enemy, and the attendant subterfuges—these are all splendid stuff and we are thrilled to march in the exciting company of Gilgamesh and Enkidu. But the making and civilizing of Enkidu is a story from an earlier world, a legend of Creation, a dawn of civilization if not of history.

The deep, rich note is not struck again until the last third of the epic, when death steps into the place of creation and proves well able to support the same sonorous tonality. The two friends' defiance of the gods, which has included their slaughter of a bull expressly sent down from heaven to punish them, has resulted in the gods putting Enkidu to death and leaving Gilgamesh to weep, tear out his hair, and ponder for the first time the universal fate of man. His long journey over land and sea to visit the Noah-figure Ziusudra and demand the secret of immortality is admirably described, as is the tragedy of his return to Uruk, when, having discovered the plant of life, he is robbed of it by a serpent. But the tragedy lies in the profound change in his own nature—his gradual transformation from a fierce warrior-king into an exhausted old man, dressed in the skins of wild animals and facing into the wind and cold of his odyssey like a Lear. No other epic so carries us from youth to age, from laughter to despair, from the start to the finish of life itself, which is perhaps why no other epic enters so deeply into our hearts or speaks to us so clearly from thousands of years away.

We also feel this closeness with particular intensity because the epic never forsakes the natural and familiar elements of life. We feel, or think we feel, the very earth over which the heroes march; their walled city seems little different from the medieval type we know from old woodcuts. When Gilgamesh, who demands nothing less than immortality, is challenged sarcastically by Ziusudra to try to stay awake for a week, and promptly falls asleep instead, Ziusudra's wife bakes a loaf of bread every morning and places it by the king's head, so that when at last he awakes, seven loaves in different stages of stale-

ness show him how long he has slept:

> The loaf of the First Day
> Is like a horse's hoof;
> The loaf of the Second Day
> Is like a leather boot.
> The loaf of the Third Day
> Is dry through and through;
> That of the Fourth Day
> Moist only in the middle;
> A green mould has touched
> The loaf of the Fifth Day;
> But that of the Sixth Day
> Would bring health to the belly.
> Now comes Faraway's wife
> With the loaf of the Seventh Day
> All warm, delicious to smell.

Here is the end of heroic hope, expressed not in high-flown terms and hyperbole but in the unchanging language of the bakery.

Who were these astonishing people who speak so easily to us from so long ago? That is the very first problem of Sumerology, and no answer has been found. Nobody knows if they were of the same stock as the first primitive inhabitants of Mesopotamia, or if they were invaders from Persia or Turkey. Nor does anybody really know how much of their great epic was strictly their own; though they themselves were conquered by others, their writing and their language conquered all who came after them, so that most of the epic is inscribed in tablets of about 2000 to 1500 B.C., when they themselves had ceased to exist. Some Sumerologists are tempted to attribute many of the episodes in the epic—the visit to Ziusudra is one of them—to Semitic successors of the Sumerians, basing their case on circumstantial evidence and theoretical argument. But this fiddling with the hour of the dawn is a risky business. We may be sure that thousands of clay tablets are still buried in the Sumerian areas of Mesopotamia, ready to go off at any moment like time bombs under many tidy theoretical arguments.

That this is likely to be the case is suggested by the record of *History Begins at Sumer*, in which the Sumerologist Samuel Noah Kramer cites in chapter after chapter the various activi-

The exploits of Gilgamesh, tamer of savage beasts, continued to be recounted by the peoples who supplanted the Sumerians. In the detail opposite, from an Assyrian relief, Gilgamesh holds, not bulls, but a lion cub.

ties in which the Sumerians could claim to be "first" (though he himself is among those who consider *The Epic of Gilgamesh* to be more a Semitic creation than a Sumerian one). To the best of our knowledge, they were the first to put the arch into architecture, the first to have schoolrooms and write school primers, the first to codify laws, write rules of medicine, produce an agricultural yearbook, record history, set the gods in their proper places, and describe the stages of Creation. That they were also the first poets there can be no present doubt, and when we examine the spread of their influence as far afield as Cappadocia, it is not fanciful to wonder, as some Sumerologists do, if the tale of Gilgamesh was known to the author of the *Iliad* and the *Odyssey*.

"In the beginning was the word," the Bible tells us, and this is literally true of the dawn of civilization in Sumer. First to discover the written word, the Sumerians owed all their greatness to it. Their wars were local affairs, based usually on quarrels over the water supplies. Their numbers were not large; the area in which they lived was relatively small. As Kramer remarks, their thinking was practical and not at all systematic, so they originated no philosophies and concocted no theories of living. But they fascinated the known world with their power to register in enduring symbols their acts, their thoughts, and their poetry. It is not for us to be surprised if they also used this precious discovery much as it is widely used today—to record business contracts, to register sales, to lay down the law, to make dishonest pronouncements, and to bamboozle the taxpayers.

Nigel Dennis, a poet and novelist, became interested in the ancient Epic of Gilgamesh *while living in the Near East. His novel* Cards of Identity *appeared in 1955.*

The Ambassadors

"... the years have taught me how desperately human beings, particularly in later life, can try to fool themselves."

By LOUIS AUCHINCLOSS

The commonest criticism of Henry James's later novels, *The Golden Bowl* and *The Wings of the Dove,* is the one made to his face by Edith Wharton: that for all their moral beauty they are severed from the nourishing human air in which real people live and move. She claimed that he had stripped his characters of the human fringes of life and placed them in a void. Now, although I believe that this is precisely what gives these novels their greatest fascination, I have become resigned to the fact that to many cultivated readers Milly Theale and Maggie Verver are both of such exquisite sensitivity as to begin to seem the same woman. *The Ambassadors,* on the other hand, the third of the great final trio and the novel that James himself regarded as his most perfect work of art, represents a median point that can be enjoyed by all James enthusiasts, whether of the early, middle, or late styles. It is as subtle as the other two, yet the characters are as vivid and sharply differentiated as any in *The Portrait of a Lady* or *The Bostonians.* Strether, for all his febrile imagination and frantic sensitivity, is as plain as an old shoe.

I first read *The Ambassadors* when I was a sophomore at Yale, and last as I approached the age of its hero: fifty-five. I found that over the years Lambert Strether had improved in my esteem. It was not that I had not initially liked him. But at nineteen I was inclined to find him a bit naive and rather bumbling. I deplored his losing his rich fiancée and the security for his old age over so minor a question of principle as whether or not a rich young man should give up his idle expatriate existence and go home to the family business. But today I find myself more identified with the Parisian convert who renounces Mrs. Newsome and all her tribe, and I can even comprehend his theory of the "virtuous attachment." This, it may be remembered, was Strether's highly personal interpretation of the relationship between the handsome, virile Chad Newsome and the beautiful, seductive Madame de Vionnet.

It will be helpful to recall the steps leading up to Strether's adoption of his theory. James's protagonist is a childless widower of high ideals but small experience, of deep sensitivity but starved imagination, who has spent a mildly useful, mildly wasted life editing a quarterly magazine in Woollett, a Massachusetts manufacturing town, and acting as cultural prime minister to Mrs. Newsome, the awesome widow who owns both town and quarterly. As the novel opens, he is on his way to Paris to rescue her son Chad from a presumably low entanglement and bring him home to play his proper role in the family affairs. Mrs. Newsome's hand in marriage and a comfortable evening of life are to be Strether's reward—if he prove successful.

Once in Paris, however, Strether's imagination begins at last to find its long-needed nourishment. It does not need much. He feels no compulsion to make himself expert in matters of art or architecture or history. He simply takes in the sights and sounds and scents of the French capital as they strike him on his leisurely round. The smallest things delight him: a watery beer at a sidewalk café, a stroll in the courtyard of his small hotel, watching a young man idly smoking on the balcony, noting the way another enters a theatre box after the lights are down. Paris comes in through Strether's every pore, and Chad Newsome and his enchanting companion, Madame de Vionnet, love his openness to it and the benignity that he brings to his contemplation of it—and them.

But this vision of Paris is fatal to his mission. Strether finds Chad not at all depraved but wonderfully changed for the better. He is a thoroughly civilized and delightful young man with charming looks and manners and a host of admirable friends. And who has accomplished this miracle but the very friend in whom Woollett has seen the incarnation of vice? Strether, after much soul searching, tears up his instructions and begs Chad *not* to go home.

It is not simply that he wants Chad to spend his life as an elegant boulevardier. It is that Strether's vision of Paris has given him a new vision of Woollett. He has always been aware of the greed and chicanery that were at the roots of the Newsome fortune. But what he now sees is the denial of life and beauty that underlies the arid consciences of Mrs. Newsome and her daughter Sarah. Their failure to see anything but vileness in Madame de Vionnet, or meretriciousness in the French capital, is also their failure to make anything out of the business of human existence but the few paltry rules of what they choose to call right and wrong. They are children: they play at living. Paris becomes fresh air to Strether and Woollett a vacuum, and his idea of what Chad must be saved from is precisely reversed.

Yet Chad, ironically enough, has been going through just the opposite experience. He has had his fill of Paris and is already weary of his liaison. The family business now tempts his idle mind; he is almost ready to go home. His sister, who succeeds the defaulting Strether, knows her brother better than does the ambassador whom she replaces. She sees that Chad basically belongs to Woollett and that he will grace the family company and serve successfully on the boards of local cultural institutions. What future, after all, is there for him in Paris playing second fiddle to a married woman? So Strether, it turns out, has lost all for nothing. All, that is, but the vision of the richer possibilities of life that Paris has opened up to him. The novel ends on the bleak hope that this vision will sustain him in the long aftermath in Woollett without Mrs. Newsome and her quarterly.

One can readily see from this outline that James's ticklish question was how to square his hero's New England conscience. For such a man as Strether is not going to tell Chad to throw over home and mother for a French countess without something to hang his inner monitor on. It was to answer this that James invented the theory of the "virtuous attachment." Chad's friend little Bilham, seeing that Strether adores everything about Chad's French life except the central fact that Chad is sleeping with a married woman ten years older than he, deliberately deceives Strether by telling him that it is a platonic relationship. Everyone else promptly joins in this amiable conspiracy of mild deceit, and Strether, adding the fervent wish to what he considers the beautiful thought, happily adopts the theory. Ultimately, he encounters Chad and Madame de Vionnet in a secluded country spot under circumstances that do not permit the survival of his illusion, but this is only after he has irrevocably broken with Sarah and lost forever his Woollett future.

Now this, when I was a sophomore, seemed to me to make Strether a bit of

an ass. Could a man of his age really for a minute believe that the relationship between a healthy American male of twenty-eight and a beautiful, sophisticated French countess would be apt to be "virtuous"? Certainly none of the Woollett characters think so. Certainly none of the Paris characters think so. And James even shows a bit what he himself thinks in the laughing rejoinder given by Miss Barrace to Strether's question about Chad and Madame de Vionnet, which she deliberately misconstrues as addressed to the "virtue" of the attachment existing between herself and a particular gentleman: "Ah, don't rob it of *all* romance!" Strether's position is ludicrous. Why in God's name should Chad stay on in Paris, giving up career, home, and marriage to dance attendance on an older woman who won't even go to bed with him?

Yet the years have taught me how desperately human beings, particularly in later life, can try to fool themselves. Strether has fallen in love with Paris and with the love that exists between Chad and Madame de Vionnet. He has never felt such exaltation before, and it is necessary for him to put it on some kind of a basis that he can understand. There is in him a stubborn, transcendental idealism that, if quixotic, is still finer than the coarser idealism of Mrs. Newsome. For all the latter's high-mindedness, she is quick to assume that Madame de Vionnet is not even the apology for a decent woman. Strether wears his New England conscience with a difference. Where Mrs. Newsome tends to condemn, he tends to extenuate. Because he sees Chad made over by a wonderfully civilized woman, he must reject the idea that they could have the kind of liaison that he has always associated with less wonderful changes in young men. To put things in his own special kind of high order he must adopt the premise that the attachment is virtuous.

It is pathetic; it is ridiculous; it is untrue. Yet, it is all the same an integral and lovable part of Strether's way of thinking and of his amiable sublimity. He has to blind himself to believe it, but he is surrounded by friends who love

him and want him to be pleased. They play along with his curious delusion. But as soon as he has seen Chad and Madame de Vionnet in the country, he knows the game is up, and he casts his little theory away in good spirit, if ruefully, even conceding that he has been a bit of an old fool. And it does not make any difference in his decision. He still advises Chad that he should not desert the woman who has so transformed him. He prefers Chad in adultery to Chad in Woollett. He does not care that the young man may be giving up a career to remain tied to the apron strings of his French mistress. But if this seems a bit strong, even to the modern reader, there *is* an extenuating circumstance. Strether knows that Chad will go back. He simply wants him to stay a little longer, to stay as long as he can, to spare Madame de Vionnet as much as possible of the agony that is inevitably in store for her. There will be plenty of time for Woollett.

Strether's own future, as envisioned in the final chapter, should theoretically not be bleak. After all, he is possessed of a new philosophy of life's possibilities. But both at nineteen and at fifty-five it seemed to me that this was going to be rather cold comfort for a lonely, aging man in Woollett, on a small income, deprived of the patronage of the Newsomes. Why must he go back? James himself seems to waver for a moment on this. Maria Gostrey, the infinitely sympathetic old maid who knows everything about Americans in Europe and who has fallen in love with Strether, offers him her hand and her beautiful little apartment in Paris. Why should he not take them? For no reason except that he is a character and she a novelist's device, what James calls a *ficelle*. Her role is to elicit facts and opinions from Strether for the instruction of the reader. She cannot marry him because she does not really exist. James sternly thrusts aside the poor *ficelle* who has struggled out of her category and sacrifices Strether to the perfect symmetry of his most perfect plot.

Though Louis Auchincloss has written no fewer than twenty-two books, this essay marks his first appearance in HORIZON.

Go and Catch a Falling Remark

Most people love wandering through strange cities: Paris is my own favorite, and San Francisco, if only for its superb situation, comes next. Some people, though not very many, enjoy roaming through unfamiliar parts of their home towns. At one time or another I have idled along nearly every street in Manhattan, constantly finding something curious or diverting—a shop selling love-potions and magical equipment, the headquarters of an organization investigating unidentified flying objects, a group of Albanian stores and eating houses. It is a pleasant way to pass time.

But what do you do when you journey day after day along the same streets? Subway to office; office to restaurant for lunch; restaurant to bank and back to office; office to subway. . . . Well, if you don't mind spending a few extra minutes, it is an excellent idea to try to vary your route every day: zigzag or make detours. Most people, however, prefer the shortest line between two points, and then what do they do? The men look at the girls; the girls look at the girls; all look at the shopwindows; and nearly all stare at the occasional kooks and freaks, loping along in fancy dress like Dr. Falke in *Die Fledermaus*, who walked home from a ball in broad daylight dressed as a gigantic bat, "to the delight of all the street urchins."

I have devised a new pastime for—one can't say "streetwalkers," "strollers" now means vehicles for transporting small children, and the French *flâneurs*, which is exactly right, sounds affected outside of France. Anyhow, a new pastime, harmless and costfree. Instead of looking at other people, listen to them. Of course, I do not mean put them under surveillance or eavesdrop on an entire conversation. Far from it. The point of this game is to catch a single fleeting remark, a floating fragment of dialogue, and then let it flutter around in your imagination. People in the streets talk freely to one another, with no idea that they can be overheard. Therefore they will say the most absurd and memorable things, and as you pass you can often pick up just a few meaningless but meaningful words.

The other day I stopped on Madison Avenue in the fifties, waiting for the green light. Two men came up on one side of me, two girls on the other. Thinking of something else, I did not even try to listen. But just as the light changed, one of the men said very earnestly, "We can get the second million from Switzerland," while one of the girls, giggling, remarked, "And then she married the *other* one!" You fill in

the rest. Again, on Park Avenue at 49th Street a fat man said (almost in my ear), "Hundreds of thousands of dollars of insurance, and not worth a nickel!" while a moment later a pretty but rather harried-looking women bent over a little boy of five and answered him, "But, darling, *both* your daddies love you!" Now and then these flying splinters are a little more pointed. In a voice like a load of gravel sliding into an excavation, "Illegal it may be; impossible it's not" (Sixth Avenue and 47th). With an accent as smooth as Jello, "Leather underwear, for Godsake, looked like a scuba diver!" (Third and 52nd).

People who speak a foreign language usually assume that no one can understand them in a strange country. I know a lady, born and brought up in Argentina, who gave up traveling on the New York subway because she could not endure the comments made about her face and figure by men who thought she knew no Spanish. Walking near the United Nations one Sunday, I saw an elegant couple in their early forties approaching: handsomely dressed, with an air that stamped them as members of the diplomatic world. They looked serenely self-possessed, strolling along in untroubled silence. However, just as they reached me, the man turned to the woman and said, almost spat out, "*¡Dinero! ¡Dinero! ¡Siempre dinero!*" —"Money! Money! Always money!" She did not even tilt her head.

Once you get your ear accustomed to picking up scraps, you can play the game almost anywhere. Wandering through working-class London, I went into a pub. As I pushed open the swinging doors there was a great burst of laughter, and then, just before I ordered my pint of mild-and-bitter, a great voice said, "Old Sam! What a card 'e was! Walked dahn Covent Garden wiv nuffin on 'im but 'is truss!"

It is difficult, but rewarding, to try this kind of phrase-grabbing at cocktail parties. As well as the fluent and energetic conversation of the woman I have just been unintelligibly introduced to, I usually get four or five broken messages from behind and from both sides. Thus, she will be telling me what is fundamentally wrong with Lincoln Center, and at the same time I hear ". . . he told her he would kill her and he damn near did . . ." and ". . . owes money to everybody in the publishing business . . ."

One of Homer's immortal clichés is "winged words." Phrases like these are winged words. They fly around like butterflies, and it is fun to snag them as they pass. Some of the butterflies may have a sting, but it is not meant for you.

By GILBERT HIGHET